George

THE LADY JULIAN

ENGLISH THEOLOGIANS
Editors—S. L. OLLARD, M.A.
W. SPENS, M.A.

THE LADY JULIAN
A PSYCHOLOGICAL STUDY

BY
ROBERT H. THOULESS, M.A., Ph.D.
FELLOW OF CORPUS CHRISTI COLLEGE, CAMBRIDGE; LECTURER IN
PSYCHOLOGY AT THE UNIVERSITY OF MANCHESTER; AUTHOR OF "AN
INTRODUCTION TO THE PSYCHOLOGY OF RELIGION"

LONDON
SOCIETY FOR PROMOTING
CHRISTIAN KNOWLEDGE
NEW YORK AND TORONTO : THE MACMILLAN CO.
Printed in Great Britain

First published 1924

PREFACE

THE present work is an attempt to study the Lady Julian from the point of view of a Christian modern psychologist. A more purely psychological treatment of the problems of mysticism and a fuller outline of the point of view from which I have approached them has been attempted in an earlier book.[1] In the present book I have quoted freely from Miss Grace Warrack's edition of Lady Julian's work,[2] but since neither citation nor exposition can adequately replace the original, it is to this work itself that I would wish to direct any of my readers whom I have managed to interest in Lady Julian. My thanks are due to the Rev. F. G. Chevassut and to my wife for their kindness in reading my manuscript and proofs, and to Dr. J. T. Mac-Curdy and the editors of this series for valuable criticism. The quotations and use of Miss Grace Warrack's work are by kind permission of the author and Messrs. Methuen & Co., Ltd., the publishers.

R. H. THOULESS.

CORPUS CHRISTI COLLEGE, CAMBRIDGE.
October 1st, 1923.

[1] *An Introduction to the Psychology of Religion* (The University Press, Cambridge, 1923).

[2] *Revelations of Divine Love* recorded by Julian, Anchoress at Norwich, edited by Grace Warrack (Messrs. Methuen & Co., Ltd., London, 1901).

CONTENTS

THE LADY JULIAN

CHAPTER I

THE MYSTIC OF NORWICH

LITTLE apology is needed for introducing the Lady Julian into a series of books dealing with English Divines. Amongst our theologians she would indeed have no place. But the development and enrichment of English religion have not resulted from the labours of theologians alone. It also owes an inestimable debt to those souls, more creative than intellectual, who have made their religion an art rather than a science. Amongst such Julian holds a high place.

An explanation may, perhaps, reasonably be expected from one who undertakes to increase the already enormous literature of mysticism. A constant danger threatens works like the present, that they should succeed only in ministering to that spurious culture which is obtained by reading only books about books. No reading of books about great works of literature and religion can take the place of the study of those works themselves. If, therefore, the present book leads its readers to turn to the work of Julian herself, it will have served a useful purpose ; if it leads them to be satisfied that they know all about her without having taken the trouble to read her, it will have done them an injury.

There are several different ways in which the writer of a book about a mystic may treat his subject. Each has its own peculiar advantages and limitations. If the writer is not a mystic himself, so that he is deprived of the possibility of an inside experimental knowledge of what he is writing about, he is left with the choice of any of the infinite number of possible points of view between two opposite extremes. One of these extremes is the point of view of the uncritical receiver of the mystics' teachings who would exalt them into a theological system. The other is that of the scientific psychological investigator to whom they are merely interesting mental phenomena possessing no defensible claim to any relationship with a reality outside the mystic's own mind.

The sympathetic attitude which results from the adoption of the first point of view is an advantage so clear that we may easily forget its real dangers. The sentimental, intellectually hazy rhapsody on mysticism written by one who is not himself a mystic does not even succeed really in being fair to the mystic. It is a transformation into realities for the intellect of all men of what are realities for the feeling of the mystic. In the passage from feeling to intellect the mystic's revelation takes on a hardness which it had not for himself. It tends to become dogma which has not the justification of traditional dogma that it is crystallised out of the experience of a community. It begins by being only (what it should have been allowed to remain) individual experience whose value lay rather in its rich feeling content than in anything which could remain to it after its intellectual formulation.

The situation is worse when the spurious mysticism of such a writer is combined with a spurious science of sentimental psychology. It is hoped in some vague way to explain the experiences of the mystics without undervaluing them by reference to a " transcendental faculty " and to " uprushings of the subliminal "— a faculty and a kind of subliminal of which the scientific study of the human mind has found no trace. This may indeed be due to the primitive condition of the science of psychology. It is possible that one day we may be able to detect the uprushing of a subliminal in contact with realities of which the conscious mind knows little ; and we may find it necessary to reinstate the faculties with the addition of a new one operative in mystical religion. But this is certainly not the case yet. With the tools of hypnosis and psychoanalysis, we seem only to discover that as we dig deeper into the mind we reach lower levels. Mysticism (like other cultures) seems to result from the utilisation for higher ends of energy derived from the lowest instincts ; it does not seem to be the welling up of something primitively exalted which has been buried beneath our conscious this-world mental activity. It is possible, but it is extremely improbable, that the psychology of the future will change all this. Until it does, it is at best confused thinking, at worst intellectual dishonesty, to use the terminology of scientific psychology, with none of its scientific meaning, to make plausible completely unscientific treatises on mysticism.

If this kind of simple credulity is not the best manner of approach to the mystic, there is also a danger in a too drastically scientific method. The scientific psychologist has a valuable weapon for the investigation of the phenomena of mysticism in the analytic method. He is, however, too easily led to suppose that this method can settle for ever all questions of the truth and value of religious revelation. The reduction of the impulses and desires of religion to transformed primitive and instinctive elements is too generally assumed to make superfluous all questions as to the reality of the objects of religion. This, however, follows from no logical necessity. It is indeed no more than a mere habit of mind. The point of view reached by an analytical psychology when applied to the study of religious experience need not be an ultimate one for deciding the question of its truth and value. For the purpose of making such a judgment, indeed, it seems to be ill suited. But if we are careful to avoid the error of thus taking it too seriously, it may be a good point of view from which to make a survey of the problems of religious experience. The psychologist is, at least, saved from the temptation to give too great an intellectual value to the emotional experiences of mysticism. Nor is he likely to use psychological terminology vaguely as a substitute for the explanation of phenomena for which no explanation can be found.

It remains the duty of one who would add to the

literature criticised in this chapter to make clear his own point of view, so that his prejudices and limitations may be apparent to his readers. The present writer is a teacher of psychology by profession, and a disciple of the Church of England to which Julian herself belonged. He is, therefore, in a favourable position to combine the faults of both of the points of view already criticised.

The aim of the present work will, however, have been fulfilled if it gives its readers a fuller knowledge and understanding with which to approach the writings of Lady Julian herself. They will find that they have come in contact with a soul of rare sweetness, a companion whose value will only increase as they become more intimate with her. In the stress and bitterness of life, they will have the consolation which can be given by the companionship of a simple and kindly lady, who can talk about God with simplicity and homeliness, because she believes that she has seen, heard, and felt the things which to us are matters only of groping speculation. The faults of the present work may be forgiven if it serves as a stepping-stone to a lasting knowledge of the immortal work of Julian herself, and introduces to new English readers the thought of one of the greatest of England's mystics.

Little is known of Julian's life. She was an anchoress living in a cell built on to the wall of the Norman church of St. Julian in Norwich. The church is used for Divine Service at the present day, and traces of the old anchorage are still to be found. She describes herself in the opening lines of her second chapter as " a simple creature that cowde no letter." The series of visions which was the occasion of her book took place on the 8th of May, 1373, when she was thirty and a half years of age, and she was still living in 1413.

The book which has given the Lady Julian a place amongst the most valued of mystical writers appears to have been completed not less than about twenty years after the actual occurrence of her revelations in 1373, although a first draft may have been written before then. Four manuscripts of her book are known, ranging in date from the middle of the fifteenth to the middle of the eighteenth century. Of these, three are in the British Museum and one in the Bibliothèque Nationale in Paris.[1] The earliest printed edition was made by a Benedictine, Dom Serenus de Cressy, in 1670, from the Paris manuscript. This was brought out in a modern edition by Fr. Tyrrell (1902). A manuscript contemporary with Julian herself was known to be in the possession of the Rev. Francis Peck, who died in 1743; but it was afterwards lost. The evidence seems to be conclusive that this is the recently discovered British Museum Additional MSS. 37790, dated 1413, which has now been printed.[2] This is much shorter than the other manuscripts. It has been suggested that it is only a part copied from the complete work, but Mr. Harford considers that it

[1] Brit. Mus., addit. MSS. 37790, Sloane 2499, and Sloane 3705; Paris, Bib. Nat., Fonds Anglais 40.

[2] *Comfortable Words for Christ's Lovers*, trans. and edited by the Rev. Dundas Harford, M.A., London.

is the earliest form of the work and that the additional material in the other manuscripts was the product of her later meditation on the subject matter of her revelations. The version from which quotations will be made in the present work is the one edited by Miss Grace Warrack from the Sloane 2499 manuscript belonging to the late seventeenth century.

The Lady Julian's book embodies an account of a number of revelations or shewings, and also the fruit of twenty years of later meditation (and, as she believed, of continued revelation) on the same subjects. The shewings did not take place without a previous mental preparation. She says that she had " afore desired three gifts of God. The First was mind of His Passion ; the Second was bodily sickness in youth, at thirty years of age ; the Third was to have of God's gift three wounds." [1] These were : " the wound of very contrition, the wound of kind compassion, and the wound of stedfast longing toward God." [2] The first petition, we may notice, was not for high mystical graces, but only for a deeper feeling in the Passion of Christ. Indeed she says explicitly : " Other sight nor shewing of God desired I never none, till the soul were disparted from the body." [3] She wished, like our Lady, and all the true lovers of Christ that saw Him on the cross, to suffer with Him. The illness, she hoped, would be so hard as to death. " I desired to have all manner of pains bodily and ghostly that I should have if I should die, (with all the dreads and tempests of the fiends) except the outpassing of the

[1] P. 3.   [2] P. 5.   [3] P. 4.

soul. And this I meant for [that] I would be purged,
by the mercy of God, and afterward live more to the
worship of God because of that sickness." [1] The first
two requests she made with the condition that they
were the will of God, but the last she asked without
condition. The first two, she says, passed from her
mind, but the third dwelled with her continually.

At the age of thirty years and a half, her desire for
bodily sickness realised itself, and she lay for several
days in an illness which appeared to be mortal. On
the seventh night of her sickness she records that she
thought it great sorrow to die, being still in youth,
not because she feared death, but because she hoped
in a longer life to have loved God better. But understanding by the feeling of her pains that she should die,
she assented fully with all the will of her heart to be
at God's will. In the morning, her curate came to
be present at her ending, and put up before her a
crucifix on which she might fix her eyes. A paralysis
and numbness which had already affected the lower
part of her body began to spread to the upper part,
her sight began to fail, and all except the Image of the
Cross seemed to be dark and horrible, as if occupied
by fiends. Then, just as she expected to pass away,
her pain was taken from her, and she was as whole as
ever before.

It then came suddenly to her mind that she should
desire the second wound, and that her body should be
filled with mind and feeling of Christ's Passion. " But
in this," she says, " I desired never bodily sight nor

[1] P. 4.

shewing of God, but compassion such as a kind soul might have with our Lord Jesus, that for love would be a mortal man : and, therefore, I desired to suffer with Him." [1] At this moment, the first of her visions started, and she seemed to see the red blood trickle from beneath the garland of thorns on the head of the Crucified. Her heart was filled with joy, and she said *Benedicite Domine* reverently and marvelling that " He that is so reverend and dreadful will be so homely with a sinful creature living in wretched flesh." [2] The visions which followed after this will be the subject of the next chapter.

Nothing is known of the details of her later life. Spent in the narrow confines of her cell at St. Julian's church, it must have been externally a very uneventful one. A window opening to the outside would enable her to speak to those who came to her, and this was practically her sole communication with the outside world. Through another window she could hear Mass and receive Communion, so keeping in touch with Christ's church on earth. In the shorter manuscript edited by the Rev. Dundas Harford, and dated 1413, it is stated that at that time the Lady Julian was still alive. [3] Therefore, she must have lived at least until the age of seventy-one ; but we have no further knowledge of the date of her death.

It is usual to speak of Julian as a religious mystic.

---

[1] P. 7.   [2] P. 8.

[3] This date was wrongly given by Blomefield in his *History of Norfolk* as MCCCCXLII instead of MCCCCXIII, which led to the belief that Julian was a hundred years old when this manuscript was written.

We must be clear about the meaning of this term, and examine the grounds on which its application to Julian may be justified.

The word *mystic* is used with many different meanings, some so wide and ill defined as to rob the word of any value as a distinguishing mark. We may, for example, call anyone a mystic who clings to beliefs because he has an inexplicable inner conviction of their truth, although this truth cannot be proved. We find, indeed, that such an attitude of adherence to unproved beliefs characterises such religious geniuses as Julian. But it is also characteristic of the people who refuse to think clearly through mere intellectual sloppiness. Some criterion of mysticism is necessary which will include this kind of religious genius, but will exclude the muddle-headed dogmatist.

In order to find such a criterion, we may study the kind of religious persons ordinarily called mystics : St. Teresa and St. John of the Cross amongst Catholics, Boehme and Law amongst Protestants, and Al-Ghazzali, the Mohammedan. We find that they do indeed assert their beliefs on the grounds of an inner conviction, rather than of any sort of external proof. Where they differ from the muddle-headed is in the fact that this emphasis does not result from the peculiar weakness of their religion on the intellectual side, but from the peculiar strength of their inner convictions. Looking at them with cold scepticism from the scientific point of view, we may decide to believe that these inner convictions are illusory ; but, at least, we must recognise that they are psychological realities. The mystic writes on religious themes with certainty, because his religious knowledge seems to come to him with the same solidity and unquestionableness as knowledge of the physical world. The objects of religion towards which the theologian reaches by intellectual speculation appear to the mystic to be given to him as actual objects of perception.

A superficial examination of mysticism might lead us to suppose that this apparent solidity of the religious knowledge of the mystic was the result of the fact that he had such abnormal experiences as visions. If the mystic seems in a vision to see the figure of Christ or a saint, it might be expected that their persons would be much more real to him than to the ordinarily religious person, who has no such experiences. But, although the mystics have often had large numbers of visions, we commonly find that they have maintained a critical attitude towards them. Visions of angels or of Christ on the Cross were often regarded by them as delusions of the Evil One, so such experiences did not in themselves give conviction of the reality of their objects. The psychological explanation of the certainty of the mystic is not such a simple one as this.

What really distinguishes the religious mystic from the ordinarily religious person is the fact that he experiences certain peculiar mental conditions in which he feels that he comes into real and convincing contact with spiritual objects. These are the mystical states of prayer, of which the most intense is the condition known as ecstasy. These states may be accompanied by visions, but also they may not. The experience of God in mystical prayer appears, from the accounts of it given by the mystics themselves, to differ in kind, and not only in degree, from such feelings of the nearness of God as occur at times to all religious persons. The words in which they describe it show that it seems to them to be something much more intimate. They tend to speak of a *possession* of God rather than a *knowledge of His presence.* The replacement of the mystic's earlier non-mystical religious experiences by the later mystical states of prayer may seem to him to be like the replacement of a state of thinking about and imagining a person by the experience of actually seeing and talking to that person. This experience is much more living and real, even if the seeing is dim, and the imagination was vivid. It is this experience of actual contact with divine things which gives to the mystical writings their peculiar manner of authoritative certainty. They are written as reports of eyewitnesses, not as the fruits of meditation or reasoning.

If we accept the occurrence of such states of prayer as our criterion of mysticism, what is our justification for calling Julian a mystic? Unlike St. Teresa and St. John of the Cross, she gives no introspective account of her methods of prayer. We have no record from herself or from anyone else that she ever experienced an ecstasy or one of the less intense forms of mystical prayer. Indeed she devotes two chapters to prayer, and talks only about the simplest kind of non-mystical prayer—the prayer of beseeching.

At the same time, we must remember that the attitude of mind which renders possible such descriptions of mental states as are to be found, for example, in the writings of St. Teresa does not belong to a primitive, unsophisticated, and childlike stage of religious feeling. It is the introspective habit of the mind— the habit of the mind looking into itself. We are not first interested in mental processes themselves, but in the things they indicate. The natural man says that he sees a horse ; with increased sophistication he may say that he has a perception of a horse. Between these two statements lies the gulf which separates the objective and the introspective attitudes of mind. On opposite sides of this gulf lie Julian's statement that she saw God in a point and St. Teresa's wonderful psychological descriptions of her states of prayer. Probably many causes combined to produce this difference in habit of mind. St. Teresa lived two centuries after Julian in more intellectual surroundings. Probably also there were innate differences. St. Teresa was a born psychologist, Julian probably a simpler and more primitive soul. We must, therefore, be on our guard against the danger of accepting the fact that Julian does not describe mystical states of prayer as evidence that she did not experience them.

Moreover, those familiar with the writings of the mystics will have no difficulty in recognising in Julian's work the characteristic features of mystical expression. She does not doubt or argue, and she speculates very little. Usually she simply affirms. Moreover, she affirms with curious confidence when she talks of things about which traditional dogma has not been confident. " The token of sin is turned to a worship " she says in the heading of her thirty-eighth chapter— a startling statement from an orthodox recluse, which is probably the best-known and most widely quoted of Julian's observations. Its bold confidence is in striking contrast with the diffidence with which she discusses such doctrines as eternal damnation, which she accepts as part of the orthodox faith, although they have not been personally revealed to her.[1] Unmistakably, her account of the objects of religion has the marks of one who feels that she has herself personal knowledge of what she is writing about. She writes in the same way as St. Teresa, St. John of the Cross, and Mme Guyon, who have given us accounts of their states of prayer, and since their condition of intimate knowledge seems to be dependent on their experience of mystical states of prayer, it is reasonable to suppose that if the Lady Julian had told us anything of her conditions of prayer we should have found that they too were mystical.

[1] See chap. xxxiii.

CHAPTER II

THE FIRST EIGHT SHEWINGS

THE revelations which form the foundation of Julian's book were communicated in various ways. Some of them were things seen with the bodily eyes or with the eyes of the mind (*visions*), others were words heard (*locutions*). There were also differences in character between different communications to the same sense. These differences followed the classical distinction between *corporeal, imaginary*,[1] and *intellectual* visions or locutions. Corporeal visions and locutions are those which seem to belong to the outside world and to be seen and heard by the bodily eyes and ears. Imaginary ones are those which seem to be of the same nature as mental images ; however vivid and striking they may be, they are in no danger of being mistaken for bodily realities. Intellectual visions and locutions are those in which, although nothing seems to be seen or heard either with the bodily sense organs or as mental imagery, there is a strong conviction of a presence or a communication. Revelations of this kind are those which persons experiencing them have found most difficult to describe. Intellectual visions

---

[1] This is a technical use of the word *imaginary*, and does not imply any criticism of the reality of the revelations concerned.

and locutions have been traditionally the most highly valued and trusted, imaginary ones less so, while corporeal visions and locutions have been treated with comparative distrust. Julian experienced all three methods of communication, and she distinguished them clearly. She does not, however, make any distinctions of value between them. She says : " All this was shewed by three [ways] : that is to say, by bodily sight, and by word formed in my understanding, and by spiritual sight. But the spiritual sight I cannot nor may not shew it as openly nor as fully as I would. But I trust in our Lord God Almighty that He shall of His goodness, and for your love, make you to take it more spiritually and more sweetly than I can or may tell it." [1] That is to say, she experienced corporeal visions, imaginary locutions, and intellectual visions. The substance of these last, she was not able to communicate ; in other words, they were ineffable. It will be remembered that William James makes ineffability (on, I think, no sufficient grounds) one of the characteristic marks of all mystical experience.[2]

The corporeal visions of Julian were mostly of scenes from the Passion. We may suppose that, in her devotions, she had long meditated on the sufferings of Christ on the Cross, and we know that she was distressed by the smallness of her feeling for His pain. She had a desire for a deeper feeling in the Passion of Christ. Although this desire passed from the

[1] P. 21.
[2] *The Varieties of Religious Experience* (London, 1907), p. 380.

conscious regions of her mind, it may well have remained as an unconscious disposition which should
determine the nature of her visions when the time was
ripe for their occurrence. This time came when she
suffered from an illness in her thirty-first year. Then
her normal mental life was weakened, and the scenes
of the Passion with which meditation had stored
her mind welled up to the surface of consciousness
and presented themselves with hallucinatory vividness.

Her revelations started when her eyes were fixed
on the crucifix, and she believed herself about to pass
away. " In this [moment]," she says, " suddenly I saw
the red blood trickle down from under the Garland
hot and freshly and right plenteously, as it were in
the time of His Passion, when the Garland of thorns
was pressed on His blessed head who was both God and
Man, the same that suffered thus for me. I conceived
truly and mightily that it was Himself shewed it
me, without any mean." [1]   Through this sight of
the blessed Passion, she felt that It was strength
enough against all the fiends of hell and ghostly
temptation.

This was clearly a corporeal vision. At the same
time, she had a shewing of our Lady which is differently
described. " I saw her ghostly, in bodily likeness
[i.e. it was an imaginary vision] : a simple maid
and a meek, young of age and little waxen above
a child." [2]

In the same time she had also a spiritual sight of

[1] P. 8.   [2] P. 9.

our Lord's homely loving. Even this more abstract object of revelation was conveyed to her mind by an image, the image of a little round thing in the palm of her hand, which she understood represented everything that was made. So little it seemed that it might have fallen to naught for littleness, were it not made to last by God's love for it.

But while she received these spiritual sights, the bodily sight of Our Lord's Passion still continued. " The great drops of blood fell down from under the Garland like pellots, seeming as it had come out of the veins; and in the coming out they were brown-red, for the blood was full thick; and in the spreading-abroad they were bright-red; and when they came to the brows, then they vanished; notwithstanding, the bleeding continued till many things were seen and understood. . . . This Shewing was quick and life-like, and horrifying and dreadful, sweet and lovely. And of all the sight it was most comfort to me that our God and Lord that is so reverend and dreadful, is so homely and courteous : and this most fulfilled me with comfort and assuredness of soul." [1]

This last thought is one on which she dwells with characteristic reverent affection. She feels that it is the highest honour a solemn King can show to a poor servant, if he will be homely with him. This marvellous homeliness is more joy to the simple soul, than if the Lord gave him great gifts and were himself strange in manner. The bodily example had been

[1] Pp. 15 and 16.

shewed " so highly that man's heart might be ravished and almost forgetting itself for joy of the great homeliness." This marvellous homeliness indeed cannot, she says, be seen in this life, except by such special shewing.

At length the bodily sight ceased, although in her heart the enlightenment remained. She desired to see more if it were God's will. Particularly now she was troubled at the apparent immediacy of her death, for she thought that the Vision was shewed for the living. She wished greatly to share with her even-Christians the comfort which her revelation had brought her. Here she breaks off the narration to exhort her readers not to give their attention to the poor creature to whom these shewings were made, but to God that of His courteous love and endless goodness would shew it generally. " For it is God's will that ye take it with great joy and pleasance, as if Jesus had shewed it to you all." [1]

Still she gazed on the face of the crucifix which was hanging before her, and again she saw with bodily sight a part of His Passion : " despite, spitting and sullying, and buffeting, and many langouring pains, more than I can tell, and often changing of colour. At one time I saw half the face, beginning at the ear, over-gone with dry blood till it covered to the mid-face. And after that the other half [was] covered on the same wise, the whiles in this [first] part [it vanished] even as it came. This saw I bodily, troublously and darkly." [2]

This second Shewing was so dim and so simple that she was troubled, doubting whether it was a Shewing. She desired more bodily sight, so that she might see more clearly. At another time she had more sight, and saw clearly that it was a shewing. " It was a figure and likeness of our foul deeds' shame that our fair, bright, blessed Lord bare for our sins : it made me to think of the Holy Vernacle [1] at Rome. . . . Of the brownness and blackness, the ruefulness and wastedness of this Image many marvel how it might be, since that He portrayed it with His blessed Face, who is the fairness of heaven, flower of earth, and the fruit of the Maiden's womb. Then how might this Image be so darkening in colour and so far from fair ? " [2] This ruefulness of our Lord's face, she explains, was the image and likeness of the shame of our sins, because He, for love of us, made Himself as like to man as He could. Even the dimness of the vision was not without symbolic meaning, for it taught that the continual seeking of the soul pleaseth God full greatly.

These bodily shewings were now interrupted by an intellectual vision (the third Shewing) in which she says that she " saw God in a Point," [3] by which sight she saw that He is in all things, and was led on to

---

[1] The handkerchief of St. Veronica with which our Lord is supposed to have wiped His face on His way to Calvary, leaving on it the impression of His features. It would seem to be from her knowledge of this cloth that the substance of the present vision is drawn. The psychologist may be interested to notice that this would correspond to the " day-remnants " in a dream.

[2] P. 23.　　　　　　　　[3] P. 26.

wonder with a soft dread : *What is sin ?* This question was raised by her mind here, because she saw that this was the point of the orthodox faith which she must grasp firmly if she were not to be carried to heretical conclusions by the implications of this vision. For she saw that God doeth " all-thing," be it never so little. This does not leave much room for sin. Indeed in the discussion of this revelation she says that she saw verily that sin was no deed. This was not, however, her last word on sin, for she decided that she would not continue to marvel about this, but would see what God would shew. The difficulty about sin was, in fact, the starting-point of a series of revelations leading to a deeper insight into the problem of sin, which may conveniently be discussed together in a later chapter.

Again the succession of corporeal visions was resumed and she " saw, beholding, the body plenteously bleeding in seeming of the Scourging, as thus :—The fair skin was broken full deep into the tender flesh with sharp smiting all about the sweet body. So plenteously the hot blood ran out that there was neither seen skin nor wound, but as it were all blood. And when it came where it should have fallen down, then it vanished. Notwithstanding, the bleeding continued awhile : till it might be seen and considered. And this was so plenteous, to my sight, that methought if it had been so in kind and in substance at that time, it should have made the bed all one blood, and have passed over about." [1] From this, she was led to describe in a passage of moving enthusiasm " the precious plenty of Christ's dearworthy blood which washes us of sin."

A pause seems to have taken place before the occurence of the Fifth Revelation (an intellectual locution). This was occupied in reflection on all that had already been seen. " Then He, without voice and opening of lips, formed in my soul these words : *Herewith is the Fiend overcome.*" [2] Julian understood that these words referred to the Passion. She saw our Lord scorn the malice of the Evil One, and set at naught his unmight, and at this sight she laughed heartily, making those around her laugh too. " And after this," she records, " I fell into a graveness, and said : *I see three things : I see game, scorn, and earnest. I see [a] game, in that the Fiend is overcome ; I see scorn, in that God scorneth him, and he shall be scorned ; and I see earnest, in that he is overcome by the blissful Passion and Death of our Lord Jesus Christ that was done in full earnest and with sober travail.*" [3]

The Sixth Revelation was also a locution. " After this our good Lord said : *I thank thee for thy travail, and especially for thy youth.*" [4] Her understanding was lifted up to Heaven, where she saw our Lord, as a lord in his own house courteously entertaining his guests. She describes the high and worshipful thanks of our Lord God to those souls who have served Him, which is part of their bliss in Heaven. " And

specially," she says, " the age of them that willingly
and freely offer their youth unto God, passingly is
rewarded and wonderfully is thanked." [1]

Her next Revelation was neither a vision nor a locution, but an alternating succession of emotional
states. First, she says, " He shewed a sovereign
ghostly pleasance in my soul. I was fulfilled with the
everlasting sureness, mightily sustained without any
painful dread. . . . This lasted but a while, and I
was turned and left to myself in heaviness, and weariness of my life, and irksomeness of myself, that scarcely
I could have patience to live. There was no comfort
nor none ease to me but faith, hope, and charity ;
and these I had in truth, but little in feeling." [2] These
opposite emotional conditions of comfort and painful
depression alternated about twenty times. The lesson
she draws from this experience is twofold. First, she
learns not to attach too much importance to feelings
of comfort or heaviness in the religious life, for loss of
the feeling of comfort does not necessarily mean that
the soul has lost its contact with God through sin,
and certainly it does not mean that God's care for it
has ceased. We must know that God " keepeth us
even alike in woe and in weal. . . . And both is one
love." [3] Secondly, she learns that it is not God's will
that we shall rest in feelings of melancholy, but that
we should overcome them. " For it is God's will that
we hold us in comfort with all our might : for bliss
is lasting without end, and pain is passing. . . . And
therefore it is not God's will that we follow the feelings

[1] P. 34.   [2] P. 35.   [3] P. 35.

of pain in sorrow and mourning for them, but that we suddenly pass over, and hold us in endless enjoyment." [1]

After this followed the most piteous of the visions of the Passion, and the one most vividly described. Indeed the pitiless realism of its description of the bodily changes accompanying the approach of death may so repel the modern reader that at this point he feels tempted to close the book of Julian's revelations and decide to read something more cheerful. He will do badly.   Julian's visions contain a deeper, truer insight into the tragedy lying on the surface of things than is to be found in the pleasant sentimentality of more conventional religious musings. It is not, indeed, their purpose to spare our feelings or her own. They had their root in a religious attitude in which was implicit the belief that sympathetic pain suffered for the pain of Christ was a good and not an evil thing, and that a genuine intuition of the joyful aspect of the Passion was conditional on a full appreciation by feeling of its physical awfulness. Some teachers of mental control at the present day teach that the highest mental advance can be attained by ceasing, as they say, to " identify," i.e. by ceasing to feel sympathetic emotions, particularly of a painful kind. Probably this is a method of attaining a certain kind of mental restfulness, though it may be at the cost of dangerous impoverishment of character. Julian invites us to the opposite course, to " identify " as completely as possible, not aiming at mental calm, but at the deepest, bitterest sympathetic pain.   She knows that

[1] P. 36.

the highest developments of character are those in which love, with its attendant pain of wide identification, is most completely exercised.

" I saw," she says, " His sweet face as it were dry and bloodless with pale dying.   And later, more pale, dead, langouring ; and then turned more dead unto blue ; and then more brown-blue, as the flesh turned more deeply dead. . . . This was a pitiful change to see, this deep dying.   And also the [inward] moisture clotted and dried, to my sight, and the sweet body was brown and black, all turned out of fair, life-like colour of itself, unto dry dying. . . . Bloodlessness and pain dried within ; and blowing of wind and cold coming from without met together in the sweet body of Christ. And these four—twain without and twain within— dried the flesh of Christ by process of time.   And though this pain was bitter and sharp, it was full long lasting, as to my sight, and painfully dried up all the lively spirits of Christ's flesh.   Thus I saw the sweet flesh dry in seeming by part after part, with marvellous pains.   And as long as any spirit had life in Christ's flesh, so long suffered He pain. . . . The sweet body was so discoloured, so dry, so shrunken, so deathly, and so piteous, as if He had been seven night dead, continually dying.   And methought the drying of Christ's flesh was the most pain, and the last, of His Passion." [1]

In this Shewing, she was led to think of the words of Christ, " I thirst."   In a later chapter she goes on to develop a deeper symbolic meaning for them in the

[1] Pp. 36 and 37.

3

Scriptural Thirst which is Christ's desire to draw us from our need up to His Bliss. At the present stage, however, she was concerned only with the surface meaning of the vision—Christ's physical pain of thirsting as he was dying on the Cross. She describes the pain of her sympathy with the agony of Christ's dying, and tells how she almost repented that she had asked for a gift so dreadful as this mental pain which seemed to pass bodily death. ". . . *Of all pains that lead to salvation this is the most pain, to see Thy love suffer. How might any pain be more to me than to see Him that is all my life, all my bliss, and all my joy, suffer?* Here felt I soothfastly that I love Christ so much above myself that there was no pain that might be suffered like to that sorrow that I had to [see] Him in pain." [1]

She felt that this was a great union between Christ and creatures that they suffered pain when He was in pain. She had a mental struggle between the impulse to look up to Heaven and to keep her eyes on the cross. This symbolised a conflict more profound than the choice between two bodily positions, for looking up from the Cross meant choosing another road to Heaven than the feeling of sympathetic pain with Christ on the Cross. So she replied : " *Nay ; I may not : for Thou art my Heaven. . . .* For I would liever have been in that pain till Doomsday than to come to Heaven otherwise than by Him." [2] It remained a comfort to her that she had chosen this path, and that her earlier half-repentance of her prayer for a sharing in Christ's woes had been merely a reluctance and

[1] P. 40.   [2] P. 42.

frailty of the flesh without assent of the soul. She believed, however, that this human sympathy with the physical sufferings of our Lord, though a necessary part, was only a part of the full understanding of the Passion. Two other manners of beholding the Passion were developed in the following shewing.

CHAPTER III

THE LAST EIGHT SHEWINGS

THE vision of Christ dying on the Cross was one of intense pain, and it was followed by an emotional reaction in the next—the Ninth Shewing—which was a joyful one, although still concerned with the Passion. The change began at the end of the Eighth Shewing, while she was still gazing at the changing body of Christ on the Cross, and expecting to see it all dead. Then His face changed, and " The changing of His blessed Countenance changed mine, and I was as glad and merry as it was possible. Then brought our Lord merrily to my mind : *Where is now any point of the pain, or of thy grief ?* And I was full merry." [1] This, she understood, was as it will be at the end of life, when those who have been with Him in His pains will suddenly have all their pains turned to joy by the changing of His Cheer to them (by their seeing the other aspect of His Passion). If they had this experience now, no pain could hurt them. It is withheld from them, so that by this suffering they can attain to a high knowledge of God which would otherwise be impossible. And the harder their pains have been

[1] P. 45.

36

with Him on the Cross, the greater shall be their worship in His Kingdom.

" Then said our good Lord Jesus Christ : *Art thou well pleased that I suffered for thee ?* I said *Yea, good Lord, I thank Thee ; Yea, good Lord, blessed mayst Thou be.* Then said Jesus, our kind Lord : *If thou art pleased, I am pleased : it is a joy, a bliss, an endless satisfying to me that ever suffered I Passion for thee ; and if I might suffer more, I would suffer more."* [1] Now she has passed beyond the simple compassionate way of regarding the sufferings of Christ, and reached the idea, central in much mystical thought, of the possible supreme worth of pain—" *the love that made Him to suffer passeth as far all His pains as Heaven is above Earth.* For the pains was a noble, worshipful deed done in a time by the working of love : but Love was without beginning, is, and shall be without ending." [2]

One of the features of Julian's mystical writings which gives them their rare charm is well illustrated in this passage. There is a friendliness and intimacy in God's speech to her, which she is glad to display. She makes, however, no suggestion that this shewed any particular regard for her, but that it is a quality of God—His " homeliness "—which presumably would be present in all His direct communications to mankind. Her attitude is as remote as possible from that of certain mystical writers whose revelations are of Christ's unique regard for their own persons. Their recitals are, indeed, coupled with protestations of their unworthiness of this honour, but the reading of

[1] Pp. 46 and 47.　　　　[2] P. 48.

them leaves a flavour in the mouth of the ordinary
Christian which he does not like. If he is a psychologist he may wonder whether this unique humility is
not a conscious over-compensation for its unconscious
opposite. Julian's is the true humility. Her locutions
are couched in terms of intimate affection, and she is
lost in wonder at the homeliness of God in His dealings
with man. She says little of her own unworthiness,
for it seems hardly to have crossed her mind that she
has any cause for self-esteem. " For truly it was not
shewed me that God loved me better than the least
soul that is in grace ; for I am certain that there be
many that never had Shewing nor sight but of the
common teaching of Holy Church, that love God
better than I." [1]

This locution introduces us to the second of the three
ways of beholding our Lord's Passion referred to at
the end of the last chapter. The first was the understanding of His hard pains. The second was the sight
of the love that made Him to suffer, which love passeth
all His pains as Heaven is above Earth. Julian says
even that our Lord said that if He might suffer more,
He would suffer more. The third way of beholding
the Passion was in understanding and sharing the
Joy and Bliss which make God to be well satisfied
with us. " And all that He hath done for us, and
doeth, and ever shall, was never cost nor charge to
Him, nor might be, but only that [which] He did in
our manhood, beginning at the sweet Incarnation
and lasting to the Blessed Uprise on Easter-morrow :

[1] P. 20.

so long dured the cost and the charge about our redemption in *deed* : of [the] which deed He enjoyeth
endlessly, as it is aforesaid." [1]

She compares the action of God in the Atonement
with that of a glad giver, little concerned about the
gift, but much about the pleasure of the person to
whom it is offered. If the receiver takes the gift
gladly and thankfully, the giver takes no account of
his own cost and trouble, because of his delight at the
pleasure of the other.

In the Tenth Shewing the mood of exultation still
predominated. It was a vision of the wound in
Christ's side ; apparently an intellectual vision, for
it is not described in such a way as to suggest either
that Julian saw it with the hallucinatory vividness of
the Shewing on the crucifix, or even that it presented
itself as a visual image at all. " Then with a glad
cheer," she writes, " our Lord looked unto His Side
and beheld, rejoicing. With His sweet looking He
led forth the understanding of His creature by the
same wound into His Side within. And then he
shewed a fair, delectable place, and large enough for
all mankind that shall be saved to rest in peace and
in love. . . . And with the sweet beholding He shewed
His blessed heart even cloven in two. And with this
sweet enjoying, He shewed unto mine understanding,
in part, the blessed Godhead, stirring then the poor
soul to understand, as it may be said, that is, to think
on, the endless Love that was without beginning,
and is, and shall be ever. And with this our good

[1] P. 50.

Lord said full blissfully : *Lo, how that I loved thee. . . .* This shewed our good Lord for to make us glad and merry." [1] We may notice in this Revelation, as in earlier ones, a curious concreteness in the objects of Julian's shewings. She sees the heart of Christ cloven in two. In such a shewing as this might be hidden the seeds of a concrete devotion to the Sacred Heart. The sight of Christ's heart is clearly a symbolisation of His love for mankind, and one is led to wonder why it was necessary for this idea to undergo such symbolisation. Is there not possibly some fundamental difference between the mind of Lady Julian and that of the reader who finds it necessary to translate her symbolism back to its abstract form before her revelation is really intelligible to him ? This is a question into which we will go more deeply in the next chapter.

The Eleventh Shewing was a ghostly sight of our Lady Saint Mary, " high and noble and glorious, and pleasing to Him above all creatures." Julian expected to have seen her in bodily presence, but saw her not so. From which, she says, " am I not learned to long to see her bodily presence while I am here, but the virtues of her blessed soul : her truth, her wisdom, her charity ; whereby I may learn to know myself and reverently dread my God." [2] This was the third time that our Lady had been shewn. During the first shewing, Julian had had an intellectual vision of her as when she was with child, during the eighth Revelation as she was in her sorrows under the Cross, and here she appeared as she is now in pleasing, worship, and joy.

[1] Pp. 51 and 52.   [2] P. 53.

Again our Lord appeared, more glorified than she had seen Him before, and taught her that " our soul shall never have rest till it cometh to Him, knowing that He is fulness of joy, homely and courteous, blissful and very life. Our Lord Jesus oftentimes said : *I it am, I it am : I it am that is highest, I it am that thou lovest, I it am that thou enjoyest, I it am that thou servest, I it am that thou longest for, I it am that thou desirest, I it am that thou meanest, I it am that is all. I it am that Holy Church preacheth and teacheth thee, I it am that shewed Me here to thee.*" [1] These were some only of the words which she heard Him speak to her. Others she found herself unable to tell, and these seemed to her to be the highest, but the joy that she saw in the shewing of them passed, she says, all that heart may wish for and soul may desire. So, although they could not be declared by her, she prays that every man after the grace that God giveth him in understanding and loving, may receive them in our Lord's meaning.

Then she began to wonder " why by the great fore-seeing wisdom of God the beginning of sin was not letted : for then, methought, all should have been well. This stirring [of mind] was much to be forsaken, but nevertheless mourning and sorrow I made therefor, without reason and discretion. But Jesus, who in this Vision informed me of all that is needful to me, answered by this word and said : *It behoved that there should be sin ; but all shall be well, and all shall be well, and all manner of thing shall be well.*" [2] In this Shewing, she was filled with Christ's compassion for the sins of her fellow Christians, as before she had been filled with His pain on the Cross, for she saw them " shaken in sorrow and anguish, tribulation in this world, as men shake a cloth in the wind. And as to this our Lord answered in this manner : *A great thing shall I make hereof in Heaven of endless worship and everlasting joys."* [1] But the words of this revelation intensified Julian's perplexity on the subject of sin instead of removing it. She beheld things generally, troublously and mourning, asking with full great dread : " *Ah ! good Lord, how might all be well, for the great hurt that is come by sin, to the creature ? "* [2] These reflections on sin and the succession of locutions on this subject which make up the Thirteenth Revelation are described in fourteen chapters of Julian's book, so it will be convenient to mention them here only shortly, and to discuss them more fully in a later chapter.

During the course of them she hoped to have full sight of Hell and Purgatory, but of these she saw nothing beyond her earlier revelation of the reproval and endless condemnation of the devil. In all this she was in no wise drawn from the orthodox faith, but understood that she was unwisely turning her attention to a question whose solution held no profit for her spiritual advancement. " And as long as we are in this life, what time that we by our folly turn us to the beholding of the reproved, tenderly our Lord God toucheth us and blissfully calleth us, saying in our soul : *Let be all thy love, my dearworthy child :*

[1] P. 58.   [2] P. 60.

turn thee to Me—I am enough to thee—and enjoy in thy Saviour and in thy salvation.'' [1]

The Fourteenth Revelation was also a locution, and was on the subject of prayer. Julian had experienced the feeling of barrenness in prayer, when it seems to the one praying that God does not hear, for no emotion is felt. " And all this," she says, " brought our Lord suddenly to my mind, and shewed these words, and said : *I am Ground of thy beseeching : first it is My will that thou have it ; and after, I make thee to will it ; and after, I make thee to beseech it and thou beseechest it. How should it then be that thou shouldst not have thy beseeching ?* " [2]

After a short discussion of this shewing there is, in the longer manuscripts, a considerable disquisition " anent certain points in the foregoing revelations." It is clear that this was written long after the occurrence of the revelations, for it contains references to lapses of time such as the following : " twenty years after the time of the shewing, save three months, I had teaching inwardly, as I shall tell." [3] This part is not to be found in the shorter manuscript edited by the Rev. Dundas Harford, and this fact may be evidence that it was not part of Julian's earliest account of her revelations. She insists again that her two manners of knowledge, her shewings (of the endless unblaming love of God) and the common teaching of Holy Church (of our deserving of blame and wrath for our sins) are not to be regarded as opposed to each other, but

[1] P. 74.   [2] P. 84.   [3] P. 110.

that her revelations only strengthened her faith in this common teaching. Indeed, she believes that for the understanding of her revelations it is necessary to bear constantly in mind the fact of human blameworthiness. Perhaps if this section is a later addition to her book, its purpose is in part to correct a tendency to novelty in her teachings on sin which her more mature judgment regarded as dangerous if taken without sufficient respect for the orthodox faith. Although she had no doubt that her shewings and the teaching of the Church could be reconciled, she could not at first see the manner of their reconciliation, and " could have no patience for great straits and perplexity, thinking : *If I take it thus that we be no sinners and not blameworthy, it seemeth as I should err and fail of knowing of this truth ; and if it be so that we be sinners and blameworthy,—Good Lord, how may it then be that I cannot see this true thing in Thee, which art my God, my Maker, in whom I desire to see all truths ?* " [1] She was bold to ask for this enlightenment, because it was for a low thing, common and not special, and of practical importance if she was to live in the light of her revelations and still to continue correctly to distinguish between good and evil.

In response to this desire she had a vision (partly imaginary and partly intellectual) of a Lord and a Servant which was shewn full mistily in answer to Julian's puzzlement over the dilemma that either we are not blameworthy (which she recognised as con-

[1] P. 106.

tradicted by Christian teaching) or else was mistaken in not seeing in God blame for sinful man. It is not clear from the narrative when this revelation took place, but the peculiarity of its position suggests that it was not at the same time as the other shewings. This vision is analysed with a detail which will be a joy to anyone familiar with the modern technique of dream interpretation. Its length and its subject matter make it more convenient to defer a fuller description of this important vision to a later chapter. After indicating how her great difficulty had been some deal eased by this vision, she spends several chapters in further developing the theme of the love of God for the soul, in which she speaks of God as our Mother. This curious and characteristic phase of Julian's thought may also be left to another chapter.

After this digression Julian returns to the narrative of her shewings and describes the Fifteenth Revelation. This was in part a locution, in part a vision, both determined by her old wish to leave the world and its woe, of which, she said, if there had been none but the absence of our Lord, she thought it was " some-time " more than she might bear.

" And to all this our courteous Lord answered for comfort and patience, and said these words : *Suddenly thou shalt be taken from all thy pain, from all thy sickness, from all thy distress and from all thy woe. And thou shalt come up above and thou shalt have me to thy meed, and thou shalt be fulfilled of love and of bliss. And thou shalt never have no manner of pain,*

*no manner of misliking, no wanting of will ; but ever
joy and bliss without end. What should it then aggrieve
thee to suffer awhile, seeing that it is my will and my
worship ? . . .*

" And in this time I saw a body lying on the
earth, which body shewed heavy and horrible, without shape and form, as it were a swollen quag of
stinking mire. And suddenly out of this body
sprang a full fair creature, a little Child, fully
shapen and formed, nimble and lively, whiter than
lily ; which swiftly glided up into Heaven. And
the swollenness of the body betokeneth great
wretchedness of our deadly flesh, and the littleness
of the Child betokeneth the cleanness of purity in
the soul. And methought : *With this body abideth
no fairness of this Child, and on this Child dwelleth no
foulness of this body.*

" It is more blissful that man be taken from pain,
than that pain be taken from man ; for if pain be taken
from us it may come again : therefore it is a sovereign
comfort and blissful beholding in a loving soul that we
shall be taken from pain." [1]

The general form of this vision reminds us forcibly
of the birth symbolisation often found in dreams. In
religious literature this form is often found to convey
the meaning of spiritual rebirth.

This was the last shewing of the day. The shewings
had followed each other fairly continuously from four
until past nine. Her feeling of bodily sickness, which
had been in abeyance during this period, now returned

[1] Pp. 160 and 161.

and the spiritual comfort of her revelations also passed from her. While in this state, she at first considered that the revelations she had received were the ravings of her delirium, but she found that when she spoke of them to a religious person who visited her he received them earnestly and with great reverence. She was then much ashamed that she " for folly of feeling of a little bodily pain, so unwisely lost for the time the comfort of all this blessed Shewing of our Lord God." [1] So she lay still till night, trusting in His mercy until she began to sleep, when she was disturbed by a diabolical vision.

" . . . Methought the Fiend set him on my throat, putting forth a visage full near my face, like a young man's, and it was long and wondrous lean : I saw never none such. The colour was red like the tilestone when it is new-burnt, with black spots therein like black freckles—fouler than the tilestone. His hair was red as rust, clipped in front, with full locks hanging on the temples. He grinned on me with a malicious semblance, shewing white teeth : and so much methought it the more horrible. Body nor hands had he none shapely, but with his paws he held me in the throat, and would have strangled me, but he might not." [2]

She woke terrified by this horrible shewing, but as the persons around ministered to her, her heart began to comfort. Then she carried her mind to all the earlier shewings of that day, and to all the faith of Holy Church. " And anon all vanished away, and I was

[1] P. 165.   [2] P. 166.

brought to great rest and peace, without sickness of body or dread of conscience." [1]

The series of revelations then came to an end with an intellectual vision followed by an intellectual locution. These form the sixteenth revelation. Its subject was the worth of the human soul, and its power of overcoming the forces of evil.

" And then," she says, " our Lord opened my spiritual eye and shewed me my soul in midst of my heart. I saw the Soul so large as it were an endless world, and as it were a blissful kingdom. And by the conditions that I saw therein I understood that it is a worshipful City. In the midst of that City sitteth our Lord Jesus, God and Man, a fair Person of large stature, highest Bishop, most majestic King, most worshipful Lord ; and I saw Him clad majestically. And worshipfully He sitteth in the Soul, even-right in peace and rest. And the Godhead ruleth and sustaineth heaven and earth and all that is—sovereign Might, sovereign Wisdom, and sovereign Goodness— [but] the place that Jesus taketh in *our Soul* He shall never remove it, without end, as to my sight : for in us is His *homeliest* home and His *endless* dwelling.

" And in this [sight] He shewed the satisfying that He hath of the making of Man's Soul. . . . For I saw in the same Shewing that if the blessed Trinity might have made Man's Soul any better, any fairer, any nobler than it was made, He should not have been full pleased with the making of Man's Soul. And He

[1] P. 167.

willeth that our hearts be mightily raised above the
deepness of the earth and all vain sorrows, and rejoice
in Him." [1]

This was a delectable sight and a restful shewing.
It was followed by a locution without voice and without opening of lips in which she was reassured of the
divine origin of the earlier shewings. This was as
follows : " *Wit it now well that it was no raving that thou
sawest to-day ; but take it and believe it, and keep thee
therein, and comfort thee therewith, and trust thou thereto :
and thou shalt not be overcome.*" [2]

This was the end of the shewings, but Julian had
still to suffer one more diabolical visitation, for,
" The Fiend came again with his heat and with his
stench, and gave me much ado, the stench was so vile
and so painful, and also dreadful and travailous.
Also I heard a bodily jangling, as if it had been of two
persons ; and both, to my thinking, jangled at one
time as if they had holden a parliament with a great
busy-ness ; and all was soft muttering, so that I
understood nought that they said. And all this was
to stir me to despair, as methought—seeming to me
as [though] they mocked at praying of prayers which
are said boisterously with [the] mouth, failing [of]
devout attending and wise diligence. . . . My bodily
eye I set in the same Cross where I had been in comfort
afore that time ; my tongue with speech of Christ's
Passion and rehearsing the Faith of Holy Church ;
and my heart to fasten on God with all the trust
and the might. . . . And thus he occupied me all that

---

[1] Pp. 167 and 168.   [2] P. 169.

4

night, and on the morn till it was about prime day. And anon they were all gone, and all passed ; and they left nothing but stench, and that lasted still awhile ; and I scorned him." [1]

[1] Pp. 170 and 171.

CHAPTER IV

SOME CHARACTERISTICS OF JULIAN'S THOUGHT

BEFORE passing to a consideration of particular teachings embodied in the shewings of the Lady Julian, we may notice two characteristics of her thought which must strike at once her most casual reader. These are the rich content of imagery in her thinking, and her almost repellent insistence on the physical awfulness of the crucifixion. The former is a point of psychological interest upon which we may dwell a little ; the second is one which we shall be forced to consider, for it would be indeed useless to commend a mediæval religious writer to the average reader of the present day unless some defence could be made for her against the charge of morbidity.

The plentifulness of the imaginal content of Julian's thought is shown not only by the corporeal and other visions of her revelation. She seems at other times to think in pictures. An example of the ease with which her thought expressed itself in imagery may be found in her tenth chapter. Her mind was occupied with the abstract idea that a man or woman in any situation " if he might have sight of God so as God is with a man continually, he should be safe in body and soul, and take no harm : and overpassing, he should have more

solace and comfort than all this world can tell." [1]
This thought expressed itself in a visual image of
" the sea-ground, and there I saw hills and dales green,
seeming as it were moss-begrown, with wrack and
gravel." [2]

And later, when she received the locution, " *I
thank thee for thy travail, and especially for thy youth*,"
the thought contained in this shewing presented itself
in the following visual image : " I saw our Lord as a
lord in his own house, which hath called all his dearworthy servants and friends to a stately feast. Then
I saw the Lord take no place in His own house, but I
saw Him royally reign in His house, fulfilling it with
joy and mirth, Himself endlessly to gladden and to
solace His dearworthy friends, full homely and full
courteously, with marvellous melody of endless love,
in His own fair blessed countenance." [3] It should be
noticed that this picture of our Lord in Heaven is
not described as a shewing. It did not appear to
Julian to have come from outside herself, as did the
words of thanks. It was simply the way in which she
thought of the idea of God thanking those who have
served Him.

The significance of these observations for an appreciation of Julian's methods of thought may best be
appreciated if we examine shortly the process of
thinking as it goes on in different minds. Probably
the most primitive elements in our thinking are
images. These are pictures seen before the mind's eye,
sounds heard, movements felt in the mind, or repro-

[1] P. 22.   [2] Ibid.   [3] P. 33.

ductions of sensations from other senses (smell, taste, etc.). They may be simple reproductions of the past, or new combinations of imagined impressions—the work of the creative imagination. Such images form an undercurrent in most of our thinking, attaining a more important position in the condition of reverie, and becoming dominant in dreams. Dreams seem to be the expression in images of primitive levels of thought of which we are not conscious when, in waking life, we are dominated by our environment with its demand for action.

A later acquired element of our mental life is our habit of thinking in words. Words, when we think them, are of course also images (we must either image the movements of pronouncing them, or their sound, or their appearance), so the kinds of imagery mentioned in the previous paragraph may be distinguished by giving them the name of *concrete images*. It is mainly the use of words in thinking, under conscious direction and control, which makes up intellectual processes of thought—processes which stand at the opposite pole to mere dreaming.

In addition, however, to words and concrete images, there appear to be elements in our thought of a more elusive character which have been given the somewhat clumsy name of " imageless thought." These are immediate grasps of meanings—of relationships or of references to fact—without any appearance of a mental intermediary in the form of a word or other image. Such imageless thoughts are much more diffi-cult to speak of clearly, since they are less tangible than concrete images and words; but they are probably no less important for the full understanding of the thinking process.

Galton was the first person to draw attention to the importance of the differences between the types of thinking in different minds.[1] He found that, while most persons have more or less rich and vivid imagery of things seen, such visual imagery may be completely absent from the minds of other persons, particularly of those who have devoted themselves to abstract thought. It is difficult for the person with vivid visual imagery to imagine what a barren waste would appear to him the mind of the person without visual images ; while the verbal thinker is shocked if he discovers that the intellectual processes of the visualiser are accompanied by what seem to him to be merely a logically irrelevant riot of mental pictures. Differences of outlook are often determined by such profound differences in the contents of different peoples' minds, and the adherents of different schools of philosophy may have their views determined in this way.[2]

It is a very important peculiarity of our thinking in words that we can distinguish between valid and invalid trains of thought by logical rules. Of course, we can reach conclusions (and correct conclusions) by using images and imageless thoughts without going through

[1] *Inquiries into Human Faculty*, by Galton ; see also *Remembering and Forgetting*, by Professor T. H. Pear (London, 1922).

[2] It is probable, for example, that the difference between the nominalists and the conceptualists in the seventeenth and eighteenth senturies was essentially the difference between predominantly visual and predominantly verbal thinkers.

a logical process of reasoning. Indeed, it is probable that generally most of us reach our conclusions in this way; but we can only be sure whether such conclusions are right or wrong when they are put to the test of experience. It is only when our steps to the conclusion have taken logical verbal form that we can assure ourselves that they are right and can convince other people of their rightness before they have been tested by experience.

Most persons will agree to one limitation of verbal thinking—that it is powerless, by itself, to give us new knowledge. We may be able by the use of words to draw correct conclusions from our experience, but no manipulation of words alone can tell us anything except what those words mean in the current use of language. It can tell us nothing about facts. The belief that manipulation of words can give us new knowledge about facts is the fallacy underlying certain ambitious metaphysical theories by which men have tried to gain knowledge about the universe by *a priori* construction of theories.

Possibly there is another limitation. The biological end of our intelligence is to enable us to modify our environment for our advantage. Verbal thinking is the last and most efficient weapon for this end. Professor Bergson suggests, however, that it is not an effective method of discovering what is ultimately true. Philosophic thought was not the end for which the intelligence was designed in the course of evolution. There are conditions known to the student of religion in which verbal thinking is reduced to a minimum and its place is taken by images and the processes of imageless thought. These may be called conditions of intuitional knowledge. Such knowledge, whether true or false, may be very convincing to the person experiencing it. He cannot demonstrate to us that it is true, for it cannot be put into logical verbal form without losing its character; but we must bear in mind the possibility of such intuitional conditions giving a real insight into reality, possibly even an insight which cannot be gained by verbal thinking. Such states certainly occur in mysticism, and their occurrence produces the note of subjective certainty which was mentioned in the first chapter as a characteristic mark of mystical writings. A more detailed examination of such states would take us too far into fields which we must not explore now. Enough has, I hope, been said to indicate how a knowledge of the psychology of normal thinking can help us to an understanding of such conditions.

The predominant use of concrete imagery, which we have seen to be so characteristic of Julian's writing, is found very commonly (but by no means universally), in the thinking processes of mystics. It is characteristic of the type of mind most sharply opposed to the logical and mathematical, which thinks mainly in words. The person with the logical-mathematical kind of mind is inclined to call the imaginal mind primitive or infantile. Thinking in concrete images has certainly its own peculiar pitfalls. There is, for example, the danger of passing from a perceived loose analogy between two things to a tacit assumption of their identity. An image which serves well for the illustration of an abstract thought becomes a danger if new facts about the object of the thought are deduced from the properties of the image. Examples of such misuse of imaginal illustrations abound in the loose thinking of both popular theology and psychology. The word *subliminal*, for example, was coined for mental processes which seemed not to appear in consciousness. The word, of course, means " below the threshold," and suggests the image of a threshold beneath which something is buried. An improper use of the illustration was made as soon as people began to attach a different metaphorical meaning to the " below," and inferred that what was below the threshold was in some ethical respect inferior to what was present in consciousness.

While such dangers are ever present to the thought of the imaginal thinker, there are others to which he is less exposed than the thinker in words. He is, for example, generally more clearly conscious of the inadequacy of his means of expression. Julian, seeing God in a point, was not likely to be misled into thinking that she had obtained an adequate expression of the immanence of God. The religious philosopher, on the other hand, who has obtained a conception of the Absolute by the manipulation of thoughts expressed in words (as in the Hegelian dialectic), is less inclined to be modest about the adequacy of his formulæ.

One result of the predominance of imagery in Julian's thinking is the concreteness of the objects of her devotion. We may take, as an example, the rhapsody on the blood of Jesus at the end of the Fourth Revelation. " Behold and see ! " she exclaims, " the precious plenty of His dearworthy blood descended down into Hell and burst her bands and delivered all that were there which belonged to the Court of Heaven. The precious plenty of His dearworthy blood overfloweth all Earth, and is ready to wash all creatures of sin, which be of good-will, have been, and shall be. The precious plenty of His dearworthy blood ascended up into Heaven to the blessed body of our Lord Jesus Christ, and there is in Him, bleeding and praying for us to the Father,—and is, and shall be as long as it needeth ;—and ever shall be as long as it needeth. And evermore it floweth in all Heavens enjoying the salvation of all mankind, that are there, and shall be—fulfilling the number that faileth." [1] Here it is to the blood of Christ, a concrete imaginable thing, that she gives the emotional significance which to a theological mind would appear properly to belong to the notion (unimaginable and expressed inadequately in words), of Christ's Atonement. We are reminded of the devotion of St. Francis to the Christmas crib as a pictorial representation of the mystery of the Nativity. Consideration of the differences between the kind of thinking which goes on in different types of mind—one of the most striking and significant discoveries of the empirical psychology of the end of the last century—should prepare us to view with understanding the highly concrete devotions which have

[1] P. 30.

grown up in Roman piety which seem often to the uncomprehending intellectual mind to savour of idolatry.

The worst that the intellectually disposed can think of Julian's imaginal thinking is that it is childlike. But what are we to think of the content of her terribly vivid visions of the crucifixion ? The spirit in which she broods over the sufferings of Jesus on the Cross is one with which we moderns are strangely out of sympathy. We do not hesitate to call it morbid. We no longer wish to think of such things as death and misery, but prefer to saturate our minds with wholesome ideas of health and beauty. The agonising Christ on the roadside crucifix shocks us by its cruel emotional contradiction to the beauty of the sunlit Tirolese mountain and valley in which it is set. We love living too well to wish to be reminded of death at every turn.

But it may be doubted whether our rejection of " morbidity " is entirely a gain. Death, failure, and misery become no less real because we have lost our feeling of reality about them. We may " healthy-mindedly " refuse to face the fact, but fact it remains, that the end of all our earthly struggles, hopes, and loves is death and bodily decay. We have attained " healthy-mindedness " by thrusting these facts out of the region of conscious recognition. In the rare moments of realisation when they force themselves into consciousness they are an unresolved terror before which we quail until we can again attain confidence by the redirection of our energy towards the business of living. Julian's method of dealing with the ultimate horror of existence was the opposite of this. She saturated her mind with pictures of this side of life, trying not to banish the morbid from consciousness but rather to attain the fullest possible consciousness of it, with the object of developing an attitude towards existence which should include it but in which it should be robbed of its power to terrify. This she succeeded in doing. If we do not believe in Julian's religion we shall probably say that she attained mental harmony by the construction of a delusional system. But at least we must admit that she did attain a harmony, and a harmony which was stable because it included all the facts ; while the harmony of " healthy-mindedness " is essentially unstable because it refuses to face a wide range of facts, which, as life advances, it becomes more difficult and finally impossible to continue to ignore.

Such a complete view of the universe as is contained in a religion like that of Julian is also attained by those who face the facts of pain, desolation, and hopelessness, and who find them so to predominate that any belief in a benevolent God appears to them to be impossible. Thus a modern philosopher writes : " Brief and power-less is man's life ; on him and all his race the slow, sure doom falls pitiless and dark. Blind to good and evil, reckless of destruction, omnipotent matter rolls on its relentless way ; for man, condemned to-day to lose his dearest, to-morrow himself to pass through the gate of darkness, it remains only to cherish, ere yet the blow falls, the lofty thoughts that ennoble his little

day." [1]   It is true that such a view of the universe leads
to a despairing resignation instead of to the hope of
Lady Julian, but both are alike in their " morbidity "
—in their fearless facing of unpleasant facts—and both
are equally far removed from the shallow cheerfulness
which results from the repressions of " healthy-
mindedness."

In a later chapter I shall try to demonstrate that
there is a further purpose in this close affective touch
with suffering.   This purpose is that it may take the
place, in the life of the mystic, of the pain which the
love for other persons brings to one whose affections
have remained in the world.   The love which seeks the
sky may too easily be lost in the self.   Christ in agony
on the Cross is the object calling out in sympathetic
pain all the love of Julian, thus saving her from the
dangers of self-love.

It is probably true also that the sufferings of Christ,
on which Julian's mind dwelt, themselves served to
strengthen the bond of her love for Him.   There is a
primitive element in the sex instinct which finds itself
attracted by the pain, physical or mental, of the
beloved.   Even this element is made to serve, by
devotion to Christ's Passion, a useful purpose in the
building up of Julian's religious sentiment.   Sympathetic pain, which is the sharing of the pain of a loved
one, strengthens love as no other relationship can.
From the psycho-pathological side, it is no more a
really effective criticism of religious devotion of this

[1] " The Free Man's Worship," by the Hon. Bertrand Russell,
reprinted in *Philosophical Essays* (London, 1910), p. 70.

kind to say that it is sadism, than to say that other forms
of devotion are disguised sexuality. All the elements
in our instinctive make-up can be used and transmuted
for the ends of the religious sentiment, and the more
perfectly God-directed is a person's character, the more
certain it is that they will be so used.

One must not omit to notice, also, her diabolical
visitations. These were two in number : the first
when the Fiend set him on her throat while she was
sleeping on the night following the first fifteen revelations ; the other the noise of mocking jangling after
the Sixteenth Revelation.[1] It is customary amongst
writers on this subject to apologise for the entry of
such elements in mystical revelations and to judge the
worth of a religious mystic by the smallness of such
pathological elements. I prefer to regard such phenomena as integral parts of the mystical processes, as
little pathological as the formation of sediment in the
process of maturing good wine. In any case, such terms
as *pathological* appear to be abusive epithets which do
not at all help towards understanding any psychological fact.

Let us consider the forces we may suppose to be at
work in mysticism on the human side to see if this
study supplies us with any better understanding of
the diabolical element in mystical experience. The
mechanism suggested by modern psychological knowledge is that of primitive instincts evolved for primitive
biological ends—the ego instincts for the preservation
of the individual in a largely hostile environment,

[1] These visitations are described in full in Chap. III.

the herd instincts for welding him into communities and so preserving the existence of social groups, and the sex and parental instincts for securing the continuance of the race. We see how, in the mystic's purgation each of these instincts is denied its natural outlet so that its energy may be given wholly to the religious sentiment. Julian fasted and probably practised other austerities so that her desires might be detached from her own earthly comfort and be directed entirely towards God. She lived the life of a celibate and solitary, so that neither her love for husband or children nor even her desire for human intercourse of a less intimate kind might distract her from an undivided love of God. But, since the material from which her mysticism grew was human nature with instinctive desires craving their natural biological end, these suppressed elements in her mental make-up (particularly when control was weakened by illness) tended to break through their restraint and to exhibit themselves in their simple and natural forms. These forms were to her evil because they were opposed to the supernatural redirection of her instinctive energies which was dominant in her character. Thus, primitive sexual desire remained a suppressed but not destroyed element in her psyche, and expressed itself in the vision of the young man who set him on her throat and thrust near her face a visage which was long and wondrous lean. The other elements—his red hair, his paws, and his malicious grin—which made this vision a horrible one —may be regarded as the reaction of her " higher " nature against the primitive and suppressed desires which were obtruding into her consciousness. Similarly, we may regard the noise of mockery at gabbled prayers as the expression of that part of her own nature which remained in revolt against her subjugation to the demands of the exclusive love of God. The mechanism of this visitation may well have been the same as that of the compulsions to blasphemous speech and acts which have often been the torment of persons of saintly life.

Instead of regarding these diabolical visitations as in themselves evidences of something unhealthy in the mysticism of those in whose lives they are found, we may consider that they show the clear-sightedness with which the mystic recognises the character of the impulses surging up from his suppressed instincts. It is an unhealthy symptom when such impulses are not recognised in their true character ; when, for example, an impulse of primitive eroticism, instead of appearing as a diabolical visitation, undergoes a merely sentimental transformation into an apparently religious experience. Such transformation is, for example, probably to be found in the stories (which offended the good sense of William James) of nuns whose spiritual experiences seem to have contained amatory embraces and expressions of personal preferences of Jesus Christ for themselves.[1] It seems reasonable to suppose that the same mental events would have led to some other (perhaps diabolical) experiences in persons more alive to their real source. Diabolical visitations, then, can be

[1] *The Varieties of Religious Experience*, chapter on " The Value of Saintliness."

regarded as the occasional activity of parts of the whole mental make-up which have been rejected by a mind dominated by the desire for the exclusive love of God. They are diabolical, not because they are evil in themselves (though indeed they may be), but because they are rejected, and are thus evil from the point of view of the mystic. Their occurrence is no measure of the unhealthiness of Julian's mysticism; rather they are a natural by-product of the whole mystical process.

CHAPTER V

THE PROBLEM OF SIN

In order to understand the Lady Julian's musings on this subject it is necessary to be clear about the exact problem which perplexed her. She was worried mainly about the problem of sin, and very little about the problem of pain. Probably this is a fundamental difference between the mediæval point of view and our own. We have at the back of our minds a conviction that the universe was created for us to be happy in, and we find it difficult to reconcile the fact that we suffer with our belief in the goodness of God. The mediæval mind had no such tender concern for human suffering. Mediæval institutions had not human happiness as their object, and they inflicted unnecessary suffering with a callousness which shows a totally different attitude towards the world from that of modern humanitarianism. Devout thinkers, such as Julian, regarded the world as a creation for the purpose of promoting the glory of God, and human beings as instruments for doing His will. They were perplexed at the difficulty of reconciling human failure to do God's will with their belief in God's omnipotence. So the problem of pain (which is so real to us that churches can be filled when a preacher promises to say some new thing about it)

66

meant little to them, while their problem of sin grows less and less oppressive to the typically modern mind.

Julian began to speculate about sin in her Third Revelation, after she had seen God in a point. " I beheld and considered, seeing and knowing in sight, with a soft dread, and thought : *What is sin ?* For I saw truly that God doeth all-thing, be it never so little. And I saw truly that nothing is done by hap nor by adventure, but all things by the foreseeing wisdom of God. . . . Wherefore me behoveth needs to grant that all-thing that is done, it is well-done : for our Lord God doeth all. For in this time the working of creatures was not shewed." [1]

For this time she was content to put the question off with a vague suggestion of the unreality of sin, a somewhat superficial solution of the problem, with which minds less insistently honest than Julian's have often remained satisfied ; and she wisely decided to cease to wonder about the problem, but to wait for a further revelation. " And here," she says, " I saw verily that sin is no deed : for in all this was not sin shewed. And I would no longer marvel in this, but beheld our Lord, what He would shew." [2]

A further difficulty was the impossibility of imagining that God could be angry, and in the fifth shewing she says : " in God there may be no wrath, as to my sight : for our good Lord endlessly hath regard to His own worship and to the profit of all that shall be saved." [3] This is difficult to reconcile with the orthodox teaching that God is angry with the sins even of those who will

---

[1] Pp. 26 and 27. [2] P. 27. [3] P. 31.

ultimately be saved (it must be remembered that Julian is never considering the others). She felt this difficulty and later it was the occasion of the shewing of the Lord that had a Servant.

Her mind reverted to the subject in her Thirteenth Revelation. She recalled the longing that she had had earlier to love God better, and saw that nothing "letted" her but sin. So she wondered why such a thing as sin had ever been allowed to exist. " And so I looked, generally, upon us all, and methought : *If sin had not been, we should all have been clean and like to our Lord, as He made us.* And thus, in my folly, afore this time often I wondered why by the great foreseeing wisdom of God the beginning of sin was not letted : for then, methought, all should have been well. This stirring [of mind] was much to be forsaken, but nevertheless mourning and sorrow I made therefor, without reason and discretion." [1]

She was answered in the words of this revelation : " *It behoved that there should be sin ; but all shall be well, and all shall be well, and all manner of thing shall be well.*" [2] The words of Jesus were spoken so tenderly, without blame to any that shall be saved, that she says later that it were " a great unkindness to blame or wonder on God for my sin, since He blameth not me for sin." [3]

It is worth noticing that it is no part of her solution of the difficulty to acquit God of the responsibility for the existence of sin. It is possible to solve the problem by regarding sin as an alien element in God's

[1] Pp. 55 and 56.   [2] P. 56.   [3] P. 57.

universe which marks a limitation of His power. This is the solution of dualism, which was boldly adopted with all its difficulties by William James. But Julian felt strongly the need for an omnipotent God, and the tendency of her thought was monistic. So this way out of the difficulty was not possible to her, and she speaks without hesitation of God having suffered sin to come. " And in these words," she says, " I saw a marvellous high mystery hid in God, which mystery He shall openly make known to us in Heaven : in which knowing we shall verily see the cause why He suffered sin to come. In which sight we shall endlessly joy in our Lord God." [1]

So far her revelations have given her nothing but a triumphant assertion of an optimistic faith in face of the apparently hopeless facts of sin. She heard the inward voice assure her that all should be well, without any explanation of how this could be. This is not a solution of her difficulties, but only an assurance that a solution was possible. Her revelations, however, did not leave the problem here. A more concrete solution was suggested in two ways. The first part of her solution was that a Great Deed would be done by Our Lord " in which Deed He shall save His word and He shall make all well that is not well." [2] The nature of this deed, she stated, could not be comprehended by our minds now, except in an element which she describes. This element is related to the conception of the *felix culpa*—that a greater good had come through sin and its forgiveness than could have

[1] P. 57.   [2] P. 67.

been known if innocence had been unsullied. This she states in a boldly original form : " In Heaven ' the token of sin is turned to worship.' "[1] It will be convenient to discuss these separately as two parts of her solution of the problem of sin—first, her faith in a deed, unexplained and essentially incomprehensible, but finally adequate ; and, secondly, the humanly understandable element in this deed, the turning to worship of the marks of sin.

Before we go on to discuss her solution of the problem of sin in more detail we may pause for a while to inquire what she meant by sin. Her life was one in which she was unusually sheltered from the fierce conflicts between duty and self-interest which occur in the life of the world, nor is it likely that she suffered much from the uncensored demands of those primitive instinctive forces which make up a large part of the conception of sin in the minds of ordinary persons. This, indeed, is clear from the text. When the sense of her teaching would comprehend *sin* in general, the particular sins which were represented to her mind were two only : " the one is impatience, or sloth : for we bear our travail and our pains heavily ; the other is despair, or doubtful dread." [2] These, she says, are they that " most do travail and tempest us, and of them would our Lord have us be amended." But she is careful to add that she is referring only to such men and women as for God's love hate sin and dispose themselves to do God's will. Such have passed beyond the stage when their moral conflict is the control of

[1] P. 77.   [2] P. 178.

earthly passions. These have been mortified, and such things as spiritual inertia and unfruitful heaviness over past sins (twin offspring of an incompletely mortified self-love), become the things against which they must struggle.

Julian's conception of sin, was, however, much wider than this, for in the Thirteenth Revelation she says : " In this naked word *sin*, our Lord brought to my mind, generally, *all that is not good*, and the shameful despite and the utter noughting that He bare for us in this life, and His dying ; and all the pains and passions of all His creatures ghostly and bodily ; (for we be all partly noughted, and we shall be noughted following our Master, Jesus, till we be fully purged, that is to say, till we be fully noughted of our deadly flesh and of all our inward affections which are not very good ;) and the beholding of this, with all pains that ever were or ever shall be,—and with all these I understand the Passion of Christ for most pain and overpassing." [1] This is a curious passage, for she is describing pains not sins. The reason for this is that she was still under the domination of the idea that sin was unreal, while the pain of which it was the cause was real. " I saw not *sin*," she says, " for I believe it hath no manner of substance nor no part of being, nor could it be known but by the pain it is cause of. And thus pain, *it* is something, as to my sight, for a time." [1]

A clearer idea of what sin meant to Julian can be obtained if we turn to the end of her discussion " Anent Certain Points " (between the Fourteenth

[1] P. 56.

and the Fifteenth Revelations), in which she talks about the unnaturalness of sin. " Sin," she says, " is in sooth viler and more painful than hell, without likeness : for it is contrary to our fair nature. For as verily as sin is unclean, so verily is it unnatural, and thus an horrible thing to see for the loved soul that would be all fair and shining in the sight of God."[1]

A better understanding of the attitude of mind which produces intense revulsion from sin while the actual sins repented of seem to be of such trivial character can be attained if we bear in mind the essential character of mysticism. This is the fact that the mystic loves God, not with the intermittent and partial fervour of the ordinary religious person, nor with the cold intellectualised love suggested by the phrase *amor Dei intellectualis*. The mystic's love is passionate, intense, absorbing, like the passionate love between a woman and a man. To understand the mystic's relationship to God, we must study what is most like it in earthly relationships—that existing between human lovers. Sin is to Julian an injury against love, an injury most unnatural because the lover would be " all fair and shining " in the sight of the loved one. She does not think of it as an infringement of a law or as something for which God will be angry. The sadness of an injury to love is the greater because the pain of the lover does not make him either angry or reproachful. So Julian feels that it would be a great unkindness to blame or wonder on God for her sins, since He did not blame her for sin.

[1] Pp. 157 and 158.

This, then, is what sin is for those that shall be redeemed—an injury to the love of God, causing grievous pain and especially the most grievous pain of His Passion. So in the course of her Thirteenth Revelation she " stood beholding things general, troublously and mourning, saying thus to our Lord in my meaning, with full great dread : *Ah ! good Lord, how might all be well, for the great hurt that is come, by sin, to the creature ?* . . . And thus our good Lord answered to all the questions and doubts that I might make, saying full comfortably : *I may make all thing well, I can make all thing well, I will make all thing well, and I shall make all thing well ; and thou shalt see thyself that all manner of thing shall be well.* . . . And thus in these same five words aforesaid : *I may make all things well,* etc., I understand a mighty comfort of all the works of our Lord God that are yet to come. There is a Deed the which the blessed Trinity shall do in the last Day, as to my sight, and when the Deed shall be, and how it shall be done, is unknown of all creatures that are beneath Christ, and shall be till when it is done." [1]

But the traditional element in Julian's religion taught her of another side of sin which seemed more hopeless of an ultimately optimistic solution than that of the sin of the redeemed ; this was the sin of the damned. " One point of our Faith is that many creatures shall be condemned : as angels that fell out of Heaven for pride, which be now fiends ; and man in earth that dieth out of the Faith of Holy Church :

[1] Pp. 60, 62, and 65.

that is to say, they that be heathen men ; and also man that hath received christendom and liveth unchristian life and so dieth out of charity : all these shall be condemned to hell without end, as Holy Church teacheth me to believe. And all this [so] standing, methought it was impossible that all manner of things should be well, as our Lord shewed in the same time." [1]

This doubt was answered by a simple reaffirmation of the assurance that all would be well : " *That which is impossible to thee,*" she was told, " *is not impossible to me : I shall save my word in all things and I shall make all things well.*" [2] She resolved both to hold the orthodox faith (as, for example, with respect to the damned), and also to hold fast to the assurance of her revelation that all things should be well. At the same time she decided to worry no more about what the Deed should be, but to desire to be like the saints in heaven, " that will right nought but God's will and are well pleased both with hiding and with shewing. For I saw soothly in our Lord's teaching, the more we busy us to know His secret counsels in this or any other thing, the farther shall we be from the knowing thereof." [3]

The lapse of time and the change of outlook do not prevent Julian's triumphant assertion that all shall be well from arousing an answering thrill of conviction in the mind of the modern reader. At all ages the human mind has had the property of responding to apparently hopeless situations by optimistic belief even on slender

[1] P. 66.   [2] P. 67.   [3] P. 69.

rational foundation. It is clear that Julian's hope is merely a dogmatic assertion on the strength of a mystical insight which can carry no intellectually grounded conviction to anyone who does not share that experience of insight. It asserts both of two intellectually irreconcilable propositions, and says that both, in some way which our minds cannot grasp, are true. This is a characteristic habit of the mystics which our over-intellectualised minds are inclined to find irritating. Yet it is not really an irrational one if the limitations of the human mind in face of ultimate reality are admitted. If ultimate facts are beyond the possibility of intellectual statement, it is not irrational to hope that a Deed shall be done which will put all things right. Clearly, being even unable to state what such a Deed could be, we are not able to prove it. But then, Julian does not claim to be able to prove the truth of her solution ; she merely asserts the substance of her own conviction. This she has a right to believe, for it is equally beyond proof and disproof. We must not forget that it is beyond disproof. The fulfilment of our deepest needs may, indeed, provide beliefs that we tend to believe on insufficient intellectual grounds. But, at least, these may be true. The fact that a belief fulfils a need is certainly, in itself, no proof of its falsity. At worst, in the face of such dark problems as those over which Julian is brooding, she and those like her may claim that they have a right to hope.

But she also specifies a part of this great Deed when she says that the tokens of sin shall be turned to worship. This, of course, applies only to the redeemed ;

she is leaving the problem of the damned on one side altogether. We can understand this hope if we remember the elements in her faith which must be reconciled. She believes that ultimately all things must be well. The sin of God's lovers, even sin forgiven by Him, would remain for ever an imperfection in what should be in eternity the stainless imperfection of their worship of Him. This imperfection would disappear if she could believe that sin was altogether an illusion. Although Julian hints more than once at this solution, it is probable that the traditional element is too strong in her religion for her to push such a view to its logical conclusion. So she must be left with the other possible solution, that, real as has been the evil of sin, it will be productive, by the action of God, of some greater good ; so that, in a future life, the tokens of sin shall be like the honourable scars of wounds received on a battle-field. She uses a variety of metaphors for sin which show how far her thought is from the conventional way of regarding it. The fall of the servant who had run to do his lord's bidding symbolised (in part) man's sin. In her reflections on the Thirteenth Revelation she speaks of sin as a sharp scourge with which man and woman is beaten, which maketh him hateful in his own sight. She seems to be thinking of sin as a misfortune rather than as a fault—a point of view not unusual amongst the mystics, with which may be compared the phase in the spiritual development of St. Catherine of Genoa when she " was incapable of recognising, by direct examination, the nature of her acts, whether they were good or bad." [1] This may be a stage of the love of God at which sin as a deliberate infringement of what is believed to be the good has disappeared ; which again should help us to understand that the moral conflict of the mystic is totally different from that of the ordinarily religious person.

Her shewing that the tokens of sin shall become worshipful is illustrated by a sight of several saints, and particularly Saint John of Beverley, who in his youth and in his tender age " was a dearworthy servant to God, greatly God loving and dreading, and yet God suffered him to fall, mercifully keeping him that he perished not nor lost no time. And afterward God raised him to manifold more grace, and by the contrition and meekness that he had in his living, God hath given him in heaven manifold joys, overpassing that [which] he should have had if he had not fallen. . . . And all this was to make us glad and merry in love." [2]

Before leaving the discussion of this revelation Julian points out and avoids a rock which endangers every attempt to secure a hopeful outlook by minimising the evil of sin. This rock is the suggestion that sin is not to be avoided but desired, if it produces good ultimately. St. Paul is faced by this danger when he teaches the forgiveness of sins through Christ's passion. " Shall I sin then that grace may abound ? God forbid." Similarly Julian says : " But now if any

---

[1] *The Mystical Element of Religion*, Baron F. von Hügel, vol. i, p. 119.
[2] Pp. 78 and 79.

man or woman because of all this spiritual comfort that is aforesaid, be stirred by folly to say or to think : *If this be true, then were it good to sin* [*so as*] *to have the more meed*,—or else to charge the less [guilt] to sin,— beware of this stirring : for verily if it come it is untrue, and of the enemy of the same true love that teacheth us that we should hate sin only for love. I am sure by mine own feeling that the more any kind soul seeth this in the courteous love of our Lord God, the lother he is to sin and the more he is ashamed. . . . For sin is so vile and so greatly to be hated that it may be likened to no pain which is not sin. And to me was shewed no harder hell than sin." [1]

The problems raised by these revelations and musings on sin were the subject of a separate vision—the example of the Lord that had a Servant. The occasion of this vision was, as we have seen, Julian's perplexity at an apparent contradiction between the substance of her revelations and the teaching of the Church. Since it is described in the digressions which follow the account of the Fourteenth Revelation in the Sloane manuscript and is absent from the shorter manuscript, it is possible that it did not occur at the same time as the other shewings. The narrative, however, does not make this matter clear. She seemed to have had revealed to her that God assigned to creatures no manner of blame. But although she found this sweet and delectable, yet she could not be fully eased because by the teaching of Holy Church she knew that sinners were sometimes

[1] Pp. 82 and 83.   [2] Chap. III.

worthy of blame and wrath. Since the first teaching
had been given to her by God Himself she must
necessarily accept it, but since the second had been
given her by Holy Church, she could not give it up.
She therefore desired earnestly to be able to reconcile
the two teachings.

Then she was shewn "full mistily" a wonderful
example of a Lord that had a Servant, of which sight
one part was shewed spiritually in bodily likeness, and
the other part was shewed more spiritually, without
bodily likeness. " For the first [part], thus, I saw two
persons in bodily likeness : that is to say, a Lord and
a Servant ; and therewith God gave me spiritual
understanding. The Lord sitteth stately in rest and in
peace ; the Servant standeth by afore his Lord reverently, ready to do his Lord's will The Lord looketh
upon his Servant full lovingly and sweetly, and meekly
he sendeth him to a certain place to do his will. The
Servant not only he goeth, but suddenly he starteth,
and runneth in great haste, for love to do his Lord's
will. And anon he falleth into a slade, and taketh full
great hurt. And then he groaneth and moaneth and
waileth and struggleth, but he neither may rise nor
help himself by no manner of way. And of all this the
most mischief that I saw him in, was failing of comfort :
for he could not turn his face to look upon his loving
Lord, which was to him full near. . . . I marvelled how
this Servant might meekly suffer there all this woe, and
I beheld with carefulness to learn if I could perceive
in him any fault, or if the Lord should assign to him
any blame. And in sooth there was none seen : for

only his good-will and his great desire was cause of his falling ; and he was unlothful, and as good inwardly as when he stood afore his Lord, ready to do his will. And right thus continually his loving Lord full tenderly beholdeth him. But now with a *double* manner of Regard : one outward, full meekly and mildly, with great ruth and pity—and this was of the first [part], another *inward*, more spiritually—and this was shewed with a leading of mine understanding into the Lord, [in the] which I saw Him highly rejoicing for the worshipful restoring that He will and shall bring His Servant to by His plenteous grace ; and this was of that other shewing.

" And now [was] my understanding led again into the first [part] ; both keeping in mind. Then saith this courteous Lord in his meaning : *Lo, lo, my loved Servant, what harm and distress he hath taken in my service for my love,—yea, and for his goodwill. Is it not fitting that I award him [for] his affright and his dread, his hurt and his maim and all his woe ? And not only this, but falleth it not to me to give a gift that [shall] be better to him, and more worshipful, than his own wholeness should have been ?—or else methinketh I should do him no grace.*" [1]

She confesses that she was not able fully to understand the vision at this time, and says that God gave her inward teaching as to its meaning for nearly twenty years. It is interesting to notice that there is an obvious interpretation of this vision which did not satisfy her. This obvious interpretation

[1] Pp. 107–109.

(which must suggest itself at once to every reader of the account) is merely a confirmation of her earlier conviction that God assigned no blame to creatures. For if the servant be taken to be Adam as representative of fallen man, the Lord is seen not to blame the servant, and from this it might be concluded that God did not blame men for their sins. But such an interpretation would not effect a resolution of the contradiction with which she started. She was satisfied that there was more in her vision than this. "For," she says, "in the servant that was shewed for Adam, as I shall tell, I saw many diverse properties that might in no manner of way be assigned to single Adam." She says also that, in spite of her further revelations, three properties of the revelation remained hid ; so she understood that every shewing is full of secret things—in other words, that while fresh analysis brings out deeper meanings from revelations, this analysis is never exhaustive.

Although Julian felt that the successful understanding of her visions was itself the result of divine leading, her actual way of finding their meaning was, as has already been suggested, not unlike certain modern methods of dream analysis. Each element of the vision was considered separately and was taken to be a symbolic representation of some idea. The meaning of the vision as a whole was discovered by fitting together the elementary ideas which were found to be symbolised by each small element of its pictorial content. In order to illustrate the method I will describe in detail the analysis of one section of her

6

vision—the Lord—and then, in order to appreciate the significance of the vision as a whole, I will go more quickly over the results of the remainder of the analysis.

First, in a preliminary attempt to reach the meaning of the vision, she says: "The Lord that sat stately in rest and in peace, I understood that He is God."[1] A further analysis is preceded by an additional description of His appearance. In order to avoid repetition, I will not give this additional description separately, but in connection with its interpretation. The words in italics are descriptive of the vision as it appeared, those in ordinary type are the underlying thoughts reached in the interpretation of the vision.

The place that the Lord sat on was barren and desert— God cannot occupy man's soul which he made to be His city, but he will prepare Himself no other place, but abides till man's soul is made fair again by the hard travail of God's Son. *The colour of his cloth was blue as azure—*betokening God's steadfastness. *The colour of his face was fair-brown, his eyes were black—*to shew His holy soberness. *The length and breadth of his garments—*betokeneth that He hath, beclosed in Him, all Heavens, and all Joy and Bliss.

The figure of the Servant was symbolic of more than one meaning, i.e. in psychoanalytic terminology, it was over-determined. "In the Servant is comprehended the Second Person in the Trinity ; and in the Servant is comprehended Adam : that is to say, All-Man."[2] These two significations of the Servant figure were represented by different elements in the vision. "By

[1] P. 111.   [2] P. 116.

the nearness of the Servant is understood the Son, and by the standing on the left side is understood Adam. . . . By the wisdom and goodness that was in the Servant is understood God's Son ; by the poor clothing as a labourer standing near the left side, is understood the Manhood and Adam. . . . The white kirtle is the flesh ; the singleness is that there was right nought atwixt the Godhead and Manhood ; the straitness is poverty ; the eld is of Adam's wearing ; the defacing, of sweat of Adam's travail ; the shortness sheweth the Servant's labour." [1]

There was a similar over-determination of the fall of the Servant, for this seemed to Julian to mean both the sin of man and the Incarnation of Jesus Christ. " When Adam fell, God's Son fell : because of the rightful oneing which had been made in heaven, God's Son might not [be disparted] from Adam. (For by Adam I understand All-man.) Adam fell from life to death, into the deep of this wretched world, and after that into hell : God's Son fell, with Adam, into the deep of the Maiden's womb, who was the fairest daughter of Adam ; and for this end : to excuse Adam from blame in heaven and in earth ; and mightily He fetched him out of hell." [2]

The key to the vision is this identification of Adam (representing mankind) with Christ in the person of the Servant, and of man's sin with the Incarnation in the Servant's fall. The interpretation of the vision is the translation of the felt significance of the identification in the pictorial language of the vision into words.

[1] Pp. 116 and 117.   [2] P. 116.

In this translation into words it becomes universally intelligible, but it may also become crude. Julian does not shrink from the task of expressing the meaning of her vision in verbal terms. " And thus hath our good Lord Jesus taken upon Him all our blame, and therefore our Father nor may nor will more blame assign to us than to His own Son, dearworthy Christ. . . . For all mankind that shall be saved by the sweet Incarnation and blissful passion of Christ, all is the manhood of Christ. . . . Jesus is All that shall be saved, and All that shall be saved is Jesus." [1]

In a later chapter a supplementary consequence of the identification of Christ and the sinning soul is deduced from the vision. This is the existence in man's soul of a perfect part which never can assent to sin, but always wills and works good. " In which Shewing I saw and understood full surely that in every soul that shall be saved is a Godly Will that never assented to sin, nor ever shall : which Will is so good that it may never will evil, but evermore continually it willeth good ; and worketh good in the sight of God. Therefore our Lord willeth that we know this in the Faith and the belief ; and especially that we have all this blessed Will whole and safe in our Lord Jesus Christ." [2]

At the end of the chapter in which the main interpretation of the vision is undertaken, there are a number of supplementary interpretations of elements in the vision, which, she says, served her as the beginning of an A.B.C. whereby she had some understanding

[1] Pp. 117 and 118.   [2] P. 127.

of our Lord's meaning. It is interesting to notice again, that she does not consider her lengthy analysis as exhaustive of the meaning of this vision. Indeed, she considers that all her shewings were full of secret things. These new interpretations, however, are connected with religious theory in general, and not with the meaning of the vision as a whole. They bear no particular relation to the interpretations which have gone before, and appear to be a later addition.

CHAPTER VI

JULIAN ON PRAYER AND ON THE MOTHERHOOD OF GOD

WHEN we come to Julian's teachings on prayer following the Fourteenth Revelation, it would be reasonable to expect to find some esoteric teaching on prayer suitable only to the condition of contemplatives. This, however, is not the case. She discusses the problems of prayer of the simplest kind, and the difficulties which might occur to the most ordinary Christian. Mention has already been made of the fact that progress in the mystical life is marked by the development of new kinds of prayer. Perhaps it will be as well, in order to form a background on which to study Julian's utterances on prayer, to mention briefly what are these conditions of *mystical prayer*. The combination of mystic and born introspective psychologist has been a rare one, so, in describing mystical prayer, we can hardly avoid using the terminology of one who combined perfectly these two characters—St. Teresa. It is necessary, however, to mention that St. Teresa founded her classifications of prayer on observations of herself, and that others have not agreed in detail with her accounts. Her sharp distinction between mystical and non-mystical states of prayer is, for example, not universally accepted, nor is her account of the *ligature* (i.e. the interference of mystical states of prayer with the ability to pray vocally).

In her well-known work, *The Interior Castle*, St. Teresa describes the states of prayer through which the soul passes to the highest mystical union under the metaphor of seven sets of mansions in a castle. The first three of these are the stages of non-mystical prayer by which from ordinary discursive meditation the mind passes to a condition of stillness and occupation with one subject, the *prayer of simplicity*. After this, at first for very short periods of time, then for longer, it enjoys mystical prayer, in which God only is present to the thoughts, in a new and intimate way. In these conditions the soul appears to itself to have loving possession of God rather than merely to be thinking about Him. She distinguishes degrees of mystical prayer (the fourth, fifth, and sixth mansions), in which there is progressively less distraction and more interference with other activities until in the condition of ecstasy the mind is entirely occupied with the experience, and the power of moving the body is lost. After this, she describes the seventh mansion, which she calls the *Spiritual Marriage*, in which the transports of ecstasy disappear, and the experience of union becomes calm and continuous, and is the inspiration of a life of activity.

While Julian's words on prayer are addressed to ordinary Christians, and deal therefore with such prayer experiences as are common to all men, there are at least suggestions in these chapters that she herself knew the experience of mystical prayer. Even those who ordinarily enjoy mystical prayer are sometimes unable to use it during long periods of dryness and are then compelled to pray vocally. It may be to such an occurrence as this that Julian is alluding in the following passage : " And sometime when the heart is dry and feeleth not, or else by temptation of our enemy,— then it is driven by reason and by grace to cry upon our Lord with voice, rehearsing His blessed Passion and His great Goodness ; and the virtue of our Lord's word turneth into the soul and quickeneth the heart and entereth it by His grace into true working, and maketh it pray right blissfully." [1] In a passage of rare beauty at the end of her description of the Fourteenth Revelation she describes unmistakably the experience of joyful possession of God which is mystical prayer. By God's drawing of the human soul to Him by love, after continuing prayer, she describes how it is led to a high, mighty desire to be all " oned " unto Him. " And then shall we, with His sweet grace, in our own meek continuant prayer come unto Him now in this life by many privy touchings of sweet spiritual sights and feeling, measured to us as our simpleness may bear it. And this is wrought, and shall be, by the grace of the Holy Ghost, so long till we shall die in longing, for love. And then shall we all come into our Lord, our Self clearly knowing, and God fully having ; and we shall endlessly be all had in God : Him verily

---

[1] P. 86. It should be noted that while mystical prayer is always without words, wordless prayer is not always mystical. The condition known as " acquired contemplation " or the " prayer of simplicity " is a wordless non-mystical form of prayer.

seeing and fully feeling, Him spiritually hearing, and Him delectably in-breathing, and [of] Him sweetly drinking.

" And then shall we see God face to face, homely and fully. The creature that is made shall see and end-lessly behold God which is the Maker. For thus may no man see God and live after, that is to say, in this deadly life. But when He of His special grace will shew Himself here, He strengtheneth the creature above itself, and He measureth the Shewing, after His own will, as it is profitable for the time." [1]

Julian thus holds out to her readers the experience which she has found to be the end of prayer ; but, un-like St. Teresa, she was not writing for those who were aspiring to be contemplatives, so she is little occupied with analysing her soul states. Perhaps we may hazard the guess that what determined the form of her advice about prayer were the questions and difficulties brought to her by the simple people who came to the window of her cell for advice and help. " Are we sure that God hears us ? " " Is it any good praying when we feel dry and left to ourselves ? " " Does not God already know what we want without our prayers to Him ? " " Why do we not always get what we ask for ? " Such questions as these seem to be the difficulties against which these revelations and the subsequent discussion of them are directed. They are not questions which would trouble the contemplative herself, for whom prayer had ceased to appear as a method of bending the divine will to human ends. For her prayer was " oneing "

[1] Pp. 91 and 92.

of the soul to God, and thanking was " truly to enjoy our Lord." And we may notice that her answers to these difficulties are given from the contemplative point of view. She can hardly sympathise with the attitude of those who are praying that their calves may thrive or that their cheeses may sell for a good price. When she illustrates her remarks by a concrete example, she supposes that one is praying for mercy and grace.

If we take Julian's teachings on prayer in the order in which they occur, we find that the first mention of the subject is in the passages following the description of the first revelation. It is occasioned by a subsidiary spiritual sight at the same time as the first revelation. The essential theme of this sight and of the reflections following it is that the love of God for us is so great that our clamorous petitions to Him are hardly necessary. In this spiritual sight of God's homely loving, " He shewed me a little thing, the quantity of an hazel-nut, in the palm of my hand ; and it was as round as a ball. I looked thereupon with the eye of my understanding : *What may this be* ? And it was answered generally thus : *It is all that is made*. I marvelled how it might last, for methought it might suddenly have fallen to naught for little[ness]. And I was answered in my understanding : *It lasteth, and ever shall* [*last*] *for that God loveth it*. And so All-thing hath the Being by the love of God." [1]

The symbolic meaning of the littleness of the ball is Julian's small valuation of created things in comparison

[1] P. 10.

with the Creator. "It needeth us," she says, "to have knowing of the littleness of creatures and to hold as naught all-thing that is made, for to love and have God that is unmade." [1] So in this littleness we see symbolically represented Julian's attitude of turning away from things, which is the beginning of mysticism. The yearning for God which is the complement of this turning away, or the positive element in the mystic's renunciation, is well expressed in a prayer which follows. "God, of Thy Goodness give me Thyself: for Thou art enough to me, and I may nothing ask that is less that may be full worship to Thee; and if I ask anything that is less, ever me wanteth,—but only in Thee I have all." [2]

The essential thing which Julian draws from this shewing is that our soul should cleave to the goodness of God. She begins by condemning the taking of many means of beseeching God, means which we use "for lack of understanding and knowing of Love." "Then," says she, "saw I truly that it is more worship to God, and more very delight, that we faithfully pray to Himself of His Goodness and cleave thereunto by His Grace, with true understanding, and steadfast by love, than if we took all the means that heart can think." [3] The means she mentions include appeals for the sake of His holy flesh and His precious blood, for the sake of His sweet Mother's love, and all help we have of special saints. She winds up the paragraph, however, with the passage: "For God of His Goodness hath ordained means to help us, full fair and many: of which the chief

[1] P. 11.   [2] P. 12.   [3] P. 12.

and principal mean is the blessed nature that He took of the Maid, with all the means that go afore and come after which belong to our redemption and to endless salvation. Wherefore it pleaseth Him that we seek Him and worship through means, understanding that He is the Goodness of all." [1]

It is rather difficult to reconcile this passage with her first reference to means. Perhaps one may be permitted to conjecture that it was a later addition in order to render less absolute her first condemnation of the methods of popular devotion. The earlier passage may be a rare example of Julian failing to enter into the point of view of the ordinary simple person. Such means, possibly superfluous to the developed religious habits of the contemplative, may be of unbounded value to the ordinary person. Perhaps the wider experience of her later life taught her to modify her first (almost harsh), judgment of popular devotional methods.

The keynote of all Julian's teaching on prayer is struck in this chapter—that it is asking of boons from a lover, not an attempt to bend a stern alien will to our needs. " For our soul is so specially loved of Him that is highest, that it overpasseth the knowing of all creatures : that is to say, there is no creature that is made that may [fully] know how much and how sweetly and how tenderly our Maker loveth us. . . . And therefore we may ask of our Lover with reverence all that we will." [2]

She prefaces this revelation by the admission that she

herself had sometimes felt as if God did not hear her because of her feeling of her own unworthiness or because she felt right naught, being as barren and dry after prayer as before. Her revelation is an answer to this feeling, but also it goes to the roots of the philosophy of prayer. The words she received were : *" I am Ground of thy beseeching : first it is my will that thou have it ; and after, I make thee to will it ; and after, I make thee to beseech it and thou beseechest it. How should it then be that thou shouldst not have thy beseeching ? "* [1] It will be seen that she is abandoning altogether the common-sense view of prayer that it is an action of our wills directed towards some modification of external events through the interposition of God's will. She believes that our desires, the prayer that springs from them, and the answer to the prayer, are all parts of one causal chain, all alike determined by the will of God. How can God fail to answer our prayers when He has made us desire what we pray for and has made us pray for it ? No doubt, if she were questioned, she would say that this was only true when our desires were purified, when we were truly Christ's lovers; but, even so, if pressed to their logical conclusion, the words of this shewing seem to come perilously near to making the religious person a God-directed automaton. But, of course, Julian would not so press them. Because she has no doubts about the orthodox doctrine of sin and responsibility, she is the less afraid of revelations which appear to conflict with this. We have already seen (in Chapter IV) that she did not consider it

[1] P. 84.

necessary that her body of beliefs should make a coherent whole. She was content for contradictions to remain, believing only that a fuller knowledge and understanding than we can attain to in this life would make all apparent contradictions disappear.

In studying the beliefs of a mystic, one must not forget that they are not entirely the product of mystical insight. Julian was an orthodox daughter of the Holy Catholic Church, and inherited a body of belief which reacted on her mystical revelation. Her feeling for the Church is often expressed in the course of her revelations. In her digression " Anent Certain Points " she says : " And He willeth that we take us mightily to the Faith of Holy Church and find there our dearworthy Mother, in solace of true Understanding, with all the blessed Common. For one single person may oftentimes be broken, as it seemeth to himself, but the whole Body of Holy Church was never broken, nor never shall be, without end. And therefore a sure thing it is, a good and a gracious, to will meekly and mightily to be fastened and oned to our Mother, Holy Church, that is, Christ Jesus." [1] This previously existing body of belief, held with so much firmness, may be called the " traditional element " in Julian's belief. Its importance as a stabilising influence in preventing her opinion from being fluid to every impulse of her own changing feeling, and its value in keeping her in touch with " all the blessed Common," can only be estimated by comparing her sane and conservative mysticism with that of one who was not so grounded

[1] P. 154.

and has become lost in subjectivism and peculiarity of belief.

The traditional element in Julian's religion has affected her revelations in two ways. First, by modifying the form of her revelations, and, secondly, by making it necessary for her to reconcile with orthodox belief the more original elements in them. It is hardly necessary to give illustrations of the way in which orthodox belief has influenced the form of her revelations, for this influence goes through the whole of her work. They are revelations of Christ, of His Mother, and of the Devil, all conceptions supplied by orthodox Christian teaching. Particularly we may notice the conventional character of the scenes from the Passion represented in her earlier visions. It seems reasonable to suppose that these were supplied by her familiarity with the pictures of the Passion in illuminated religious books.

The fact that her revelations were not entirely drawn from conventional orthodoxy, and might have a tendency which would need reconciliation with orthodox belief, is first suggested in her thoughts on the thirteenth revelation, in which she had the assurance that all things should be well. " And in this sight," she says, " I marvelled greatly and beheld our Faith, marvelling thus : Our Faith is grounded in God's word, and it belongeth to our Faith that we believe that God's word shall be saved in all things ; and one point of our Faith is that many creatures shall be condemned : as angels that fell out of Heaven for pride, which be now fiends ; and man in earth that dieth out of the Faith

of Holy Church : that is to say, they that be heathen
men ; and also man that hath received christendom and
liveth unchristian life and so dieth out of charity : and
all these shall be condemned to hell without end, as
Holy Church teacheth me to believe. And all this
[so] standing, methought it was impossible that all
manner of things should be well, as our Lord shewed
in the same time." [1] To this she had no other answer
in shewing, but the words : *" That which is impossible
to thee is not impossible to me : I shall save my word in
all things, and I shall make all things well."*

A little later she was again made slightly uneasy as
to the tendency of her revelations, although this was
only through an omission and not, as before, the threat
of a serious contradiction. In her further discussion
of the same shewing, she says : " For though the
Revelation was made of goodness in which was made
little mention of evil, yet I was not drawn thereby
from any point of the Faith that Holy Church teacheth
me to believe. For I had sight of the Passion of Christ
in diverse Shewings,—the First, the Second, the Fifth,
and the Eighth—wherein I had in part a feeling of the
sorrow of our Lady, and of His true friends that saw
Him in pain ; but I saw not so properly specified the
Jews that did Him to death. Notwithstanding I
knew in my Faith that they were accursed and condemned without end, saving those that converted, by
grace. And I was strengthened and taught generally
to keep me in the Faith in every point, and in all as I had
before understood : hoping that I was therein with the

[1] P. 66.

mercy and the grace of God ; desiring and praying in my purpose that I might continue therein unto my life's end." [1] The truth probably is that this evil which she saw not properly specified could not be made a felt reality for her because it did not fit in altogether consistently with her feeling about the Passion. This, to her, was a triumph over evil and sorrow, but if there were persons connected with it who must suffer sorrow and be immersed in evil eternally something would be felt to be lacking in the wholeness of this triumph. So, although she cannot feel intuitively this eternal partial success of evil, she accepts it intellectually on the authority of the Holy Church.

Indeed the doctrine of hell and eternal damnation is very generally the testing point for the traditional element in the mystic's religion. There is much that is common in the mental attitudes of all mystics. All tend to affirm a completely happy outcome of the world process, and all tend to believe that God's Being is so all-inclusive that any apparent contradictions to it (such as is provided by the reality of evil in eternity or even in time) must be an illusory appearance. If these feelings are expressed in doctrinal form, the first will probably, the second certainly, come into conflict with orthodox teaching. It is clear that we cannot both state that everything is a manifestation of the Being of God (which is the tendency of the mystical revelation), and that evil is an eternal reality opposed to His nature. Human sympathy is so all-

[1] P. 68.

inclusive as to make it difficult for most persons to
regard an outcome of the world process which involves
the eternal misery of a large number of persons
(however wicked they may have been) as an altogether
happy one. But the intuitive belief in a completely
satisfactory issue of the world process can be content
with nothing less.

So in two ways the tendency of the mystic's beliefs
comes in conflict with orthodoxy. It is interesting to
notice how different mystics deal with this conflict.
They may abandon orthodoxy and affirm the reality
of their mystical intuition, or they may refuse to allow
any weight to their intuitions unless they are con-
formable to the teachings of the Church. The first is
the way of many unorthodox mystics ; its disadvantage
lies in the fact that a steady anchor in the firm ground
of some tradition is necessary to stop the mind from
a mere wild following of every intuition. The second
is the way recommended by such mystical theologians
as Father Poulain. But Julian had too firm a faith
in Holy Church to resolve her conflict in the first way,
and too firm a faith in God's revelation to her to
resolve it in the second way. Two alternatives remain.
It is possible to state both opposed beliefs, and to say
that both are true although in the imperfect state of
our knowledge they appear now to contradict each
other. This is a perfectly reasonable position, however much it may be despised by intellectualists.
The other is to attempt a reconciliation by developing
the implications of both and seeing whether there
is not some third possibility which, being true,

would make both rivals possible. This is the way of synthesis. As we have already seen in Chapter III, Julian used both of these methods to resolve her difficulty. The shewing of the Lord that had a Servant is an instructive example of how a further revelation has developed from the impact of an earlier revelation on the rock of the traditional element in her belief.

It is interesting to notice that exactly this same conflict between what appears as a mystical insight (whether well founded or not) and the orthodox doctrine of damnation is found even in the mysticism of other religions. The Sufi mystics of Mohammedanism discussed the question, and Abdu'l-Karím ibn Ibráhím al-Jílí taught that all men would ultimately be saved, as well as that there would be special ameliorations of their temporary punishments in hell (particularly for Jews and Christians), an opinion as unorthodox in his religion as it would have been in mediæval Christianity.[1]

We have already mentioned two places in which Julian speaks of the experience of dryness and barrenness in prayer. She refers again to this subject in the chapter in which she describes the motherhood of God. She speaks of the soul realising its falling and wretchedness and, being sore adread, running to God like a child to its mother, and asking for help and grace. " And if we feel us not then eased forthwith, be we sure that He useth the condition of a wise mother.

[1] *Studies in Islamic Mysticism*, by Dr. R. A. Nicholson (Cambridge, 1921).

For if He see that it be more profit to us to mourn and
to weep, He suffereth it, with ruth and pity, unto the
best time, for love.   And He willeth then that we use
the property of a child, that evermore of nature trusteth
to the love of the mother in weal and in woe." [1]

This acceptance with full trust of spiritual desolations
is a part of the mystical life as characteristic and as
well worthy of our attention as its divine visions and
consolations.   Mere satisfaction with sensible divine
favours and resting in them is no very high spiritual
attainment.   The soul is weaned from dependence on
such consolations by the experience of abandonment
and apparent loss of divine favour.   It will be remembered that this was the lesson taught to Julian by her
Seventh Revelation, in which, after a high and confident
sense of gladness, she found herself in utter heaviness
with no feeling of the faith and love which she retained
in fact.   The lesson of this repeated experience she
took to be the necessity for retaining an even
confidence in joyful and miserable states of mind, for
" God willeth that we know that He keepeth us even
alike secure in woe and in weal." [2]   She realised the
value of the sentiment for the Church as a safeguard
against the danger of ineffective despondency to which
we are exposed if we measure our spiritual attainments
by our own individual feelings.   In the passage quoted
above, she exhorts the soul in danger of despair through
the feeling of abandonment to repair mightily to the
faith of Holy Church, which, as the body of Christ,
never has been or can be broken.

[1] P. 154.   [2] P. 35.

The feeling of dependence, hinted at in the above expressions of the relationship between the soul and God in terms of that existing between a child and its parent, is one which has long been recognised as characteristic of the religious attitude. The psychoanalysts point out the connection between the attitude of dependence and the actual emotional attitude of the child towards its parents, and explain its presence in religion as due to a return of the adult to the infantile way of feeling, with the objects of religion taking the place of the parents. Indeed some regard this return as so fundamental to religion that they suppose all religious behaviour and feelings to be made up wholly of the behaviour and feelings belonging to such a child-like attitude. Thus Dr. Jung says : " The benefits of religion are the benefits of parental care upon the child ; its mystic feelings are the unconscious memories of the tender emotions of the first childhood. . . ." [1] Without going so far as Dr. Jung, who would claim that religion is wholly made up of this element, we may readily admit that experience shows much of the individual's attitude towards the objects of his religious feeling to be determined by his relationship to his parents. A strong desire for parental authority (caused perhaps by the unsatisfactoriness or the early death of the actual father) may produce a craving for absolute authority which leads to the adoption of the creed of a religious body claiming infallibility. A similar failure of the love of his mother may lead the individual to a strong devotion to

[1] *Psychology of the Unconscious*, p. 99 (London, 1916).

some religious object towards which feelings belonging to the mother may be directed, possibly the Blessed Virgin. Suppressed hostility against the parents probably often produces those adolescent changes of religion which seem to have as their principal end a change from the religion which was received in childhood.

One may recognise the importance of this element in religion without falling into the psychological error of supposing that it makes up the whole of the mental basis of religion, or into the philosophical error of supposing that it in any way makes the reality of the objects of religion less probable. It may be, indeed, that the craving for God is something more fundamental underlying the adult craving for the parent, and that the neurotic person whose emotional life is disordered through a craving for the parental love which has been denied him since he left childhood is really suffering from the misunderstood and misdirected religious impulse. This craving may be what has been called the " religious instinct," which is directed backwards towards the parents of childhood because it has missed its true object—God.

Julian recognises very clearly this yearning of child towards parent in religious feeling. Generally she speaks of the second person of the Trinity as our Mother, very rarely of our Lady or the Church. " I understood," she says, " that the high Might of the Trinity is our Father, and the deep wisdom of the Trinity is our Mother, and the great Love of the Trinity is our Lord : and all this have we in Nature and in the making of our Substance. And furthermore I saw that the Second Person, which is our Mother as anent the Substance, that same dearworthy Person is become our Mother as anent the Sense-soul." [1] " This fair lovely word *Mother*," she says later, " it is so sweet and so close in Nature of itself that it may not verily be said of none but of *Him* ; and to her that is very Mother of Him and of all. To the property of Motherhood belongeth natural love, wisdom, and knowing ; and it is good : for though it be so that our bodily forth-bringing be but little, low, and simple in regard of our spiritual forthbringing, yet it is He that doeth it in the creatures by whom that it is done . . . thus He is our Mother in Nature by the working of Grace in the lower part for love of the higher part. And He willeth that we know this : for He will have all our love fastened to Him." [2] " Fair and sweet," she says again, " is our Heavenly Mother in the sight of our souls ; precious and lovely are the Gracious Children in the sight of our Heavenly Mother, with mildness and meekness, and all the fair virtues that belong to children in Nature. . . . And I understood none higher stature in this life than Childhood, in feebleness and failing of might and of wit, unto the time that our Gracious Mother hath brought us up to our Father's Bliss. . . . And then shall the Bliss of our Mother, in Christ, be new to begin in the Joys of our God." [3]

The looseness with which Julian uses her symbolism —which should warn us against the danger of reading into it a rigid system—is illustrated by an earlier

[1] P. 145.   [2] P. 151.   [3] Pp. 158 and 159.

passage in which she speaks, in the same breath, of God as our Father, our Mother, and our Spouse. " And thus I saw that God rejoiceth that He is our Father, and God rejoiceth that He is our Mother, and God rejoiceth that He is our Very Spouse and our soul is His loved Wife." [1]

Already we have seen one of the rare references to the Blessed Virgin as our Mother, where she speaks of " her that is very Mother of Him and of all." She speaks more emphatically later, when she says : " Thus our Lady is our Mother in whom we are all enclosed and of her born, in Christ (for she that is Mother of our Saviour is Mother of all that shall be saved in our Saviour) " ; but she closes the sentence with a curious reversion to her earlier symbol of Christ as Mother, " and our Saviour is our Very Mother in whom we be endlessly borne, and never shall come out of Him." [2] In the Eleventh Revelation, Julian had seen our Lady Saint Mary " high and noble and glorious, and pleasing to Him above all creatures," [3] but it is in a different aspect, little and simple, that she appeared in earlier revelations. " A simple maid and a meek, young of age and little waxen above a child . . . marvelling with great reverence that He would be born of her that was a simple creature of His making," [4] above all others in worthiness and grace, because of her meekness in wisdom and truth. It is not as the great Mother and the Queen of Heaven that she is here presented, but as the simple peasant girl of

[1] P. 122. [3] P. 53.
[2] Pp. 139 and 140. [4] P. 9.

Bethlehem. While Julian's sentiment for the Blessed Virgin is strong and deep, as one loved singularly by Jesus Christ, above all creatures, this sentiment does not take the central place that it came to take later in devotional literature.

CHAPTER VII

THE TRANSFORMATION OF LOVE

THE frequent failure of psychologists to attain even a moderately sympathetic understanding of the driving forces behind the mystical life is illustrated by a singularly superficial account of them which has been given and quoted with approval. This account states that the mystic from the beginning desires the pleasures of the ecstatic condition, and, through long desiring of them, finally realises them by a process of auto-suggestion. While this statement is certainly condemned by the psychological insufficiency of the second part, even its first part cannot be commended as a model of sympathetic appreciation of human motives. It is worthy to be ranked with the profound opinion that the motivation of ordinary religion is self-interest operated by the desire for heaven and the fear of hell. Nor is this opinion supported by an unbiassed examination of the facts. We do not find the mystic in the earlier stages of his career brooding over the spiritual pleasures which he is later to experience. Rather he seems to be acted on by a force of love which drives him to renounce the desire for joys earthly and heavenly, and even to welcome spiritual desolation, when it comes, as part of the discipline which weans him from the desire for pleasures. He is inclined to fear the advent of spiritual comfort, for he is afraid that the pleasure he derives from it may tempt him from the path he has chosen.

We are told, for example, that St. Catherine of Genoa fled from consolations and would say to her Lord : " I do not want that which proceedeth from Thee, but I want Thee alone, O tender Love." [1] Walter Hilton, too, finds a criterion of genuine mystical experience, not in its sensible consolations, but in its impulsion of the soul to virtue. He says : " . . . If it be so that this manner of feeling let not thy heart from spiritual exercises, but maketh thee more devout, and more fervent to pray, more wise to think ghostly thoughts, and though it be so that it astonish thee in the beginning, nevertheless afterward it turneth and quickeneth thy heart to more desire of virtues, and increaseth thy love more to God and to thy neighbour, also it maketh thee more humble in thy own eyes—by these tokens mayest thou know that it is of God." [2]

In the same spirit Julian values spiritual comforts little in comparison with an increase of love. She says after the First Revelation : " Because of the Shewing I am not good but if I love God the better : and in as much as ye love God the better, it is more to you than to me. . . . For truly it was not shewed me that God loved me better than the least soul that is in grace ; for I am certain that there be many that never

[1] *The Mystical Element of Religion*, by Baron F. von Hügel (London, 1909), p. 139.
[2] *The Scale of Perfection*, Book I, Pt. I, chap. ix.

had Shewing nor sight but of the common teaching of Holy Church, that love God better than I." [1] Her refusal to rest merely in the pleasurable emotional side of her experiences has saved her from the danger of valuing herself because of them above the more ordinary religious believers.

She knew also periods of dryness and spiritual abandonment, and accepted them as parts of her spiritual experience, necessary elements in the progress of Christ's lovers. In her Seventh Revelation, when, after being " fulfilled with the everlasting sureness " she was turned and left to herself in heaviness and weariness of her life, without comfort or ease, she commented on this experience : " This Vision was shewed me, according to mine understanding, [for] that it is speedful to some souls to feel on this wise : sometime to be in comfort, and sometime to fail and to be left to themselves. . . . And for profit of man's soul, a man is sometime left to himself ; although sin is not always the cause : for in this time I sinned not wherefore I should be left to myself—for it was so sudden. Also I deserved not to have this blessed feeling. But freely our Lord giveth when He will, and suffereth us [to be] in woe sometime. And both is one love." [2] One could hardly misunderstand the way of the mystic worse than by supposing it to be a mere seeking after sensuous religious pleasures. This is not the way of human lovers ; still less is it the way of divine lovers.

If we wish to understand the mystical life there is a good deal in modern scientific psychology which may

[1] P. 20.　　　　　　　[2] P. 35.

help us in this attempt. We are taught to attach importance to the conflict between the impulses of love and of self-interest, or, in other words, between object-love and self-love. The failure to adapt oneself satisfactorily to life by finding another person to love tends to make the energy of love turn back to the individual himself. This is called *introversion*.[1] If the attitude of introversion is over-developed it leads to the ineffectiveness and moral narrowness characteristic of the sentiment of self-love, and it may end in a form of insanity in which there is a complete withdrawal of the mind from the interests of the external world.[2]

It will be a great help towards the understanding of the struggles of the mystic if it is borne in mind that mystical religion, too, starts by a withdrawal of the energy of love from the outside world. " Made to love much," writes the biographer of Madame Guyon, " and, finding nothing to love around her, she gave her love to God." [3] A constant danger to which the mystic is exposed is that this love detached from the world may turn inwards instead of being given to God. In other words, it is the danger of unhealthy introversion. How real this danger is may be appreciated if we study the failures on the mystic way, those who have started by detaching their love from the world but

[1] I am here using the word *introversion* with the meaning which it bears in psycho-pathology. This is not the same as its usual meaning in writings on mysticism; as it is used, for example, by Evelyn Underhill.

[2] This is the form of insanity known as *dementia præcox*.

[3] *Madame Guyon*, Guerrier, p. 36.

have ended by becoming not mystics but egoists, whose religion serves the end of their own egoism. The achievement of their detachment is not humble love of God but spiritual pride, not a growth in virtue but moral deterioration. " Made to love much," might be said of them, " and, finding nothing to love around them, they gave their love to themselves."

This, then, is the practical problem of the mystic. Having withdrawn his love from objects in this world, he must save himself from the dangers of introversion by finding an object to expend it on. A religion too intellectualised will give the simple person too little to be made the object of affection. It must give him something which can be brought so near to himself that it can be made the goal of his love. This is the supreme service to the religious sentiment of the doctrine of the Incarnation, and we may see her idea of the Incarnation performing this service in the religion of Julian.

" Here I saw," she says during the course of her description of the terrible Ninth Revelation, " a part of the compassion of our Lady, Saint Mary : for Christ and she were so oned in love that the greatness of her loving was cause of the greatness of her pain. . . . For ever the higher, the mightier, the sweeter that the love be, the more sorrow it is to the lover to see that body in pain that is loved. And all His disciples and all His true lovers suffered pains more than their own bodily dying. For I am sure by mine own feeling that the least of them loved Him so far above himself that it passeth all that I can say. Here saw I a great

oneing betwixt Christ and us, to mine understanding :
for when He was in pain, we were in pain." [1]

This pain is the pain of object-love from which the
mystic can escape only at the cost of moral deterioration. In this experience, disinterested emotion for
the loved object is stronger than the emotions of self-
love. The energy of love has been given to an object
instead of being given to the self.

There are two methods in religious development,
externally so alike that they are often confused,
although in their objects they are poles apart. One
belongs to the tradition which recognises that desire
leads to sorrow and to escape sorrow teaches its disciples
to destroy desire. The other also may recognise that
sorrow is caused by desire, but does not have as its
ultimate aim the escape from sorrow. It finds a
supreme value in love, and therefore finds a value in the
pain which love brings. But this love must be detached from its earthly object and given to God. In
the one method the aim is the destruction of love, in the
other the aim is its transformation from the love of the
creature to the love of God. The first method is, of
course, that of the pessimistic Hindu systems of which
the one best known in the West is Hinâyâna Buddhism.
In such systems, the ultimate victory in the eternal
mental conflict between the self and love is given to the
impulses of self—to the forces of death. However
much alike these ascetic systems and Christianity may
appear, and however much the Christian mystic may
seem to be trying to attain the destruction of desire,

[1] P. 40.

the ultimate difference in aim must not be forgotten.
He withdraws his love from the world, but so that in
the end it may be given out again. His process of
withdrawing it is often harsh denial to himself of all
he desires on earth, the good as well as the indifferent
and evil, of the affection of his parents and friends as
well as food and drink. But he does not want to
destroy desire, he wishes to direct it all to God. Complete introversion, the *emancipation* of the oriental
ascetic, is the supreme spiritual tragedy of the Christian
mystic. There is a second stage in the asceticism of
the Christian mystic, in which the ego-impulses are
disciplined as were the love-impulses in the earlier stage.
This is the " upper school " of the spiritual life spoken
of by Suso. The discipline of desire has only put the
feet of the mystic in a road which leads equally to the
mystical love of God and to spiritual death. A more
bitter purgation is necessary by which self-love is
disciplined, so that the love which has been withdrawn
from the world may be prevented from becoming
centred on the self, and may be given passionately and
selflessly to God.

This discipline of self-love takes place in two ways :
partly by the deliberate infliction on the self of
humiliations, partly by the joyful acceptance of such
humiliations when they are inflicted by other persons or
external circumstances. Julian herself speaks of the
second of these ways. " On each person that He loveth,
to His bliss for to bring [them], He layeth something
that is no blame in His sight, whereby they are blamed
and despised in this world, scorned, mocked, and

outcasted.   And this He doeth for to hinder the harm they should take from the pomp and the vain-glory of this wretched life, and make their way ready to come to Heaven, and upraise them in His bliss everlasting.   For He saith : *I shall wholly break you of your vain affections and your vicious pride ; and after that I shall together gather you, and make you mild and meek, clean and holy, by oneing to me."* [1]

I do not wish to be misunderstood when I speak of withdrawal from the persons and things of this world as an essential step in mysticism.   It is easy to exaggerate the completeness of this withdrawal.   One may point to tender human affections amongst the mystics, and to lives of devotion to the service of their fellow men.   It is certainly true that in the late phase of the mystical life, called by St. Teresa the Spiritual Marriage and by Mme Guyon her Apostolic State, love and activity are once more given to things and persons.   The essential difference between this and ordinary this-world activity seems to be that here we find activity and love for men dominated and transfigured by the lasting union with God which is the consummation of the mystical soul's love for Him. This domination and transfiguration are the lasting results of the lower stages of the mystical way—the intermittent contemplation, and the raptures of ecstasy which have now disappeared.   It is not our business to ask whether the ecstatic condition is a desirable one or whether it is " pathological."   If, however, we find ourselves unable to resist the tempta-

[1] Pp. 58 and 59.

tion to sit in judgment on the mystics, at least let us remember that even for this-world life their experiences may be not without value ; the early emotional stages of withdrawal from the world are often means to a final phase of enriched activity.

Perhaps Julian had, at the end of her life, attained to the condition of the Spiritual Marriage ; we do not know. Certainly, anchoress though she was, hers was not a spiritual love jealously destructive of love for her fellow creatures. She asks, in her discussion of sin after her Thirteenth Revelation : " What may make me more to love mine even-Christians than to see in God that He loveth all that shall be saved as it were all one soul ? " [1] The conviction that her revelations were meant not for herself but for the world underlies all her writing, and makes the production of her book a real act of loving activity.

But such facts must not blind to the reality of the initial impoverishment of ordinary human affections which characterises the mystical life. This is a matter of simple observation, and not to be decided by our own feelings of the rightness or wrongness of such a withdrawal. It seems to be a law of human affection that love cannot be given suddenly to a new object without being withdrawn from other things (if we wish to adopt an ethical attitude towards this fact, perhaps we may call it a limitation of human nature). This is noticeably true of devotion to science, and even of ordinary love for a person of the opposite sex. One of the symptoms that a person is falling in love is the weakening of

[1] P. 76.

his affection for things he previously cared for. It is not, I think, true that love given to one thing must be withdrawn in equal amount from others, for it is equally a matter of simple observation that some manners of disposal of the affections diminish a man's whole power of loving, whereas others increase it. The mystical love of God may in the end enrich the mystic's capacity for giving love to all things. It remains true, however, that at the beginning and for very many years the claims of his love are intolerant in their demands on other affections. While true friendships are found amongst the mystics, they are, at least, rarer than amongst ordinary persons, while passionate love for a person of the opposite sex is conspicuously absent. It is true that some of the greater mystics have been married (as, for example, St. Catherine of Genoa and St. Frances of Rome), but it is only necessary to study their biographies to see that these form only an apparent exception to our rule. St. Catherine's husband was a man of low character, and her failure to find happiness in her married life because her husband was felt by her not to be a worthy or possible object of deep affection, produced the state of restlessness and conflict which terminated in her mystical conversion. St. Frances, on the other hand, although she was married and bore her husband children, had her feet already on the mystical path before her marriage, and accepted her husband in obedience to her parents as a cross to be borne for the love of God, treating him with kindness but without passion.

This impoverishment of ordinary human affections in response to the exclusive demands of the divine is responsible for an element of hardness in the mystical character in human relationships towards which the ordinary man finds it difficult to be sympathetic. A general benevolence without any passionate devotion to particular persons or things are marks of a character too cold to win general approval. When Julian asked for shewing with respect to a particular person, she found that this wish seemed to hinder insight. After the Thirteenth Revelation, " when God Almighty had shewed so plenteously and joyfully of His Goodness, I desired to learn assuredly as to a certain creature that I loved, if it should continue in good living, which I hoped by the grace of God was begun. And in this desire for a *singular* Shewing, it seemed that I hindered myself : for I was not taught in this time. And then was I answered in my reason, as it were by a friendly intervenor : *Take it GENERALLY, and behold the graciousness of the Lord God as He sheweth it to thee : for it is more worship to God to behold Him in all than in any special thing.* And therewith I learned that it is more worship to God to know all-thing in general, than to take pleasure in any special thing." [1] This is a trivial incident showing how particular affections must be sacrificed for the mystical. It may be taken as symbolic of the great sacrifices of the same kind which must have been made by Lady Julian—of the tearing apart of family ties and human friendships when she left the world to occupy her cell in St. Julian's churchyard.

[1] P. 70.

We may regard the transformation of love of which I have spoken—the redirection to God of the passions, longings, and transports of human love—as the essential factor in mysticism. We are then led to ask how such a theory helps us to orient ourselves in the facts of mysticism, and how it serves to throw light on the difference between the mystical and the ordinarily religious lives. In both classes of problem, I believe it will be found to give the truest guidance. It may be objected that to relate mysticism so closely to human love is a degradation of mysticism, and that if our conviction of the value of mysticism can be appealed to as evidence it serves to undermine the theory here suggested. But this objection seems to assume that sex-love is in itself something degraded—a view which I believe few persons would be willing explicitly to support. But it is a view so often implicit in everyday thinking and in current abuse of psychological theories that it is worth while to call attention to its falsity. The same impulse is behind the noblest human love and the lowest human degradation. The impulse itself is morally indifferent. No degradation of mysticism is implied by the view that behind it is to be found the same impulse as that of human love. We may consider that the mystical love of God is human love directed heavenwards, or that human love is the putting to a lower use of a capacity intended for the mystical employment.[1]

---

[1] The latter view is, for example, implied in Pascal's advice to his sister not to marry, because she would be giving to another what was meant for God alone.

This may be the idea contained in the following passage of Julian describing the restoration of the Sense-soul by the Incarnation of Christ. " For I saw full assuredly that our Substance is in God, and also I saw that in our sense-soul [1] God is : for in the self-[same] point that our Soul is made sensual, in the self-[same] point is the City of God ordained to Him from without beginning ; into which seat He cometh, and never shall remove [from] it . . . it behoveth needs to be that mankind shall be restored from double death : which restoring might never be until the time that the Second Person in the Trinity had taken the lower [2] part of man's nature ; to Whom the highest [3] [part] was oned in the First-making. And these two parts were in Christ, the higher and the lower : which is but one Soul ; the higher part was one in peace with God, in full joy and bliss ; the lower part, which is sense-nature, [1] suffered for the salvation of mankind." [4]

Furthermore, such a view as I have here suggested is in no way destructive of the orthodox view that the mystical graces are of a supernatural character. It is admitted by all that there is effort in the preliminary ascesis of mysticism. This ascesis I consider to be the attempt of the mystic to detach his love from objects. It may be that in a special sense divine action is needed for the final transference of the liberated love-impulse to God.

The ordinarily religious person is distinguished from the mystic (and from the Eastern ascetic who has

---

[1] " Sensualite."
[2] The Sense-soul.
[3] The Substance.
[4] Pp. 133 and 134.

attained emancipation) by the fact that he gives much more of his love still to objects, including the persons who are dear to him. Is his way of living better or worse than the mystic's ? We must not be surprised to find that the mystic often speaks as if his way of loving was the right way. He would indeed have attained a supernatural level of insight if he were free from the human failing of tending to exalt the mode of life best for himself into a universal obligation. But really it is a question about which we cannot profitably dispute. The ordinary person, equally with the mystic, must avoid the dangers of self-love by passionate and selfless devotion. Perhaps if his devotion to another person could satisfy his need for loving, his way of life would be further from that of the mystic. He approaches the mystic when he finds that the needs of his heart cannot be wholly satisfied by human love. At worst, they may not be satisfied at all ; in any case, his bonds of affection to the persons and things of this world must be broken as old age approaches. Willingly or unwillingly he must resign them, and if he is to have the peace of religious contentment at the end, it can only be by a readiness to give his heart wholly to God. Is his final surrender less valuable because he has loved life first ?

The difference between the mystical life and the perfected Christian life of the ordinary kind is ideally a difference of route rather than of goal. Complete and all-embracing love for God in response to God's love for it must be the end of every Christian soul aiming at perfection. Actually the divergence between the mystic and ordinary Christian is found to be wider than we may suppose that ideally it should be, for both fall short of perfection ; the mystic very often loves creatures imperfectly, as the ordinary Christian may love the Creator imperfectly. Even in their most perfect developments, the differences in route between the mystic and the ordinary Christian (both proceeding to the goal of perfect love) are real differences, and no good purpose is served by slurring them over. The detachment of this-world affections takes place in the mystical life by the violence of asceticism or by the willing acceptance of harsh deprivation imposed by outside circumstances. As a result of this violence of detachment, by a law of mental life (for even the mystic cannot transcend altogether the limitations of human nature), there is a profound, though perhaps not permanent, impoverishment of this-world affections. Later the mystic must avoid the danger that this love, detached from things, may become centred on the self. So far as this danger can be avoided by his own efforts, it is by meditation on the Incarnate, and by the ascesis of self-love (in which violence is done to the self-regarding sentiment and there is willing acceptance of external humiliations). A part of the mystic's reward is an early experience of divine consolations which take the place of the earthly joys he has renounced, but which he recognises as an incident rather than the goal of his quest.

The ordinarily religious person goes through no such violent detachment of his love from this world. He gives much of his love here and finds, in his this-world loves, joys and pains corresponding roughly with the consolations and the abandonments of the mystic. By no violent asceticism and by no particularly harsh deprivation is his love withdrawn from things, but in the course of his life, and increasingly as old age approaches, it suffers unavoidable deprivations. These may be accepted willingly for the love of God, or a painful state of conflict and dissatisfaction may be set up by rebellion against them. The first is the religious attitude, and this condition of willing submission to the fact that everything we value must be resigned, and that our body must be destroyed in death, is one not in the end very different from the earlier, more spectacular, renunciation of the mystic.

Certain observers who commend a temperate and adaptable religion find in the behaviour of the mystic a socially useless eccentricity of conduct bordering on mental derangement. So psychologists of religion write ponderous chapters on the question of whether " the ecstasy is a pathological condition," when they would be better employed in trying to understand mysticism instead of judging it. It must be understood that we are differently made and exposed to different circumstances. The conventional religious life of a pious woman of the world would probably have been as impossible to the Lady Julian as would have been the life of an anchoress to most of her fellows. The mystic's renunciation has, however, an heroic element in it which can compel the admiration of those who feel no call to an exact imitation of it. Even the conventionally religious are found to be willing to admit that their own is, in some sense, a lower path. It remains true that the value of the contribution of the mystics to religious thought lies in the fact that they can tell much about the goal of the religious life even to those who do not follow their route to it.

Printed in Great Britain by Hazell, Watson & Viney, Ld.,
London and Aylesbury.